CHINA-RUSSIA SECURITY RELATIONS: STRATEGIC PARALLELISM WITHOUT PARTNERSHIP OR PASSION?

Richard Weitz

August 2008

*****

*****

This manuscript was funded by the U.S. Army War College External Research Associates Program. Information on this program is available on our website, *www.StrategicStudiesInstitute.army.mil*, at the Publishing button.

*****

Comments pertaining to this report are invited and should be forwarded to: Director, Strategic Studies Institute, U.S. Army War College, 122 Forbes Ave, Carlisle, PA 17013-5244.

*****

All Strategic Studies Institute (SSI) publications are available on the SSI homepage for electronic dissemination. Hard copies of this report also may be ordered from our homepage. SSI's homepage address is: *www.StrategicStudiesInstitute.army.mil*.

*****

The Strategic Studies Institute publishes a monthly e-mail newsletter to update the national security community on the research of our analysts, recent and forthcoming publications, and upcoming conferences sponsored by the Institute. Each newsletter also provides a strategic commentary by one of our research analysts. If you are interested in receiving this newsletter, please subscribe on our homepage at *www.StrategicStudiesInstitute.army.mil/newsletter/*.

ISBN 1-58487-360-4

CONTENTS

FOREWORD

Chinese-Russian security relations directly concern many subjects of interest to the Strategic Studies Institute. These areas include regional conflicts, nonproliferation issues, and military force balances. Given the importance of these two countries in international affairs, however, almost any foreign policy action of their governments affects some American national interest.

For almost 2 decades, China and Russia have been strengthening their security ties. Nonetheless, as this monograph makes clear, the relationship between Beijing and Moscow remains in flux. In some cases, they share overlapping interests. In other instances, they compete for power and wealth, particularly for oil and gas resources.

Many factors will affect Sino-Russian ties—including developments within China and Russia as well as external events. As part of this mix, American policies will also have some impact on the future foreign behavior of both countries.

Although Washington should attempt to develop good security relations with both countries, American policymakers must also prepare to respond effectively should relations between these two great powers evolve in ways that threaten core American values and interests. This monograph suggests some policy proposals to that effect.

DOUGLAS C. LOVELACE, JR.
Director
Strategic Studies Institute

SUMMARY

Since the end of the Cold War, the improved political and economic relationship between Beijing and Moscow has affected a range of international security issues. China and Russia have expanded their bilateral economic and security cooperation. In addition, Beijing and Moscow have pursued distinct, yet parallel, policies regarding many global and regional issues. Yet, Chinese and Russian approaches to a range of significant subjects are still largely uncoordinated and at times conflict. Economic exchanges between China and Russia remain minimal compared to those found between most friendly countries, let alone allies. Although stronger Chinese-Russian ties could present greater challenges to other states (e.g., the establishment of a Beijing-Moscow condominium over Central Asia), several factors make it unlikely that the two countries will form such a bloc.

Unlike during the Cold War, China and Russia no longer fear engaging in a shooting war. For example, the two countries have largely accepted their common border. Yet, tensions persist due to illegal Chinese immigration into Russia, as well the inability of Chinese authorities to halt the spillover of pollution from China into Russia. In particular, Russians worry about the long-term implications of China's exploding population for Russia's demographically and economically stagnant eastern regions, a situation some Russian leaders already consider to be a major security threat.

In some respects, China and Russia should be natural energy partners. Chinese energy demand is soaring, and Russia's oil and gas deposits lie much closer to China than the more distant energy sources

Africa and the Persian Gulf. Nonetheless, economic and political differences relating to their energy security have continually divided the two countries, reducing the prospects for creating an exclusive energy bloc in Eurasia.

For over a decade, Russian military exports to China have constituted the most important dimension of the two countries' security relationship. Russian firms have derived substantial revenue from the sales, which also helped sustain Russia's military industrial complex during the lean years of the 1990s. China's People's Liberation Army (PLA) was able to acquire advanced conventional weapons that Chinese firms could not yet manufacture. This situation is changing. The Chinese defense industry has become capable of producing much more sophisticated armaments. Moscow confronts the choice of either seeing its Chinese market decrease dramatically or agreeing to sell even more advanced weapons to Beijing with the risk of destabilizing military force balances in East Asia.

In their public rhetoric, Chinese and Russian leaders appear the best of friends. They speak as if they share a comprehensive vision of the direction in which they want the world to evolve over the next few years. Their joint statements call for a multipolar international system in which the United Nations and international law determine decisions regarding the possible use of force. Chinese and Russian government representatives also stress traditional interpretations of national sovereignty rather than the promotion of universal democratic values or other ideologies. Yet, Beijing and Moscow continue to differ on important global issues, including ballistic missile defense (BMD) and military operations in space.

The Chinese and Russian governments have expressed concern about efforts by the United States and its allies to strengthen BMD capabilities. Their professed fear is that these strategic defense systems, in combination with strong American offensive nuclear capabilities, might enable the United States to obtain nuclear superiority over China and Russia. Despite their mutual concerns, Beijing and Moscow have never collaborated extensively in this area. For example, they have not pooled their military resources or expertise to overcome U.S. BMD technologies. Nor have they pressed in coordinated fashion other European or Asian countries to abstain from allowing U.S. BMD systems to be deployed on their soil.

As in other spheres, China and Russia have both parallel and conflicting interests in outer space. The two governments have long been concerned over U.S. military programs in this realm. In response, Chinese and Russian delegations to various UN disarmament meetings have submitted joint working papers and other proposals to begin multilateral disarmament negotiations to avert the militarization of space. In addition, Beijing and Moscow have independently issued broad threats intended to dissuade the United States from actually deploying space-based weapons. Despite their overlapping interests in countering U.S. military activities in space, Russia has been very circumspect in cooperating with China's space program. The Russian position likely reflects recognition that many aerospace technologies have direct military applications.

Central Asia perhaps represents the geographic region where the security interests of China and Russia most intersect. Their overlapping security interests have manifested themselves most visibly in the Shanghai Cooperation Organization. Yet, this harmony of interests arises primarily because Beijing deems the region a lower strategic priority than does Moscow, which still views Central Asia as an area of special Russian influence. China's growing interest in securing Central Asian oil and gas could lead Beijing to reconsider its policy of regional deference.

In East Asia, China and Russia are mutually concerned with the evolving political, military, and economic situation on the Korean peninsula, which borders both countries. In all three dimensions, the two governments have thus far pursued largely independent but parallel approaches toward both North and South Korea. In terms of influence, however, Beijing enjoys a clearly dominant role, while Moscow often struggles to maintain even a supporting position. Their policies towards Japan and Taiwan also are not well integrated. Beijing considers its ties with Tokyo and Taipei as among its most important bilateral relationships, whereas Moscow manages its relations with both states almost as an afterthought.

The limits of foreign policy harmonization between China and Russia are also visible in South Asia, where the two governments have adopted sharply divergent positions on critical issues. For instance, despite recent improvement in Chinese-Indian relations, Russia's ties with New Delhi still remain much stronger than those between China and India. Persistent border disputes, differences over India's growing security ties with the United States, competition over energy supplies, and other sources of Sino-Indian tensions have consistently impeded the realization of a possible Beijing-Moscow-New Delhi axis.

The Chinese and Russian governments have pursued parallel but typically uncoordinated policies in the Middle East. Both want to sell Iran weapons, nuclear technologies, and other products. In addition, Beijing and Moscow, though defending Tehran in the Security Council, warn against any Iranian ambitions to acquire nuclear weapons. In addition, they both opposed the U.S.-led invasion of Iraq, while sharing concerns that an early American military withdrawal from that country could lead to an increase of Islamic militarism throughout the Middle East. Thus far, however, neither country has sought to make issues related to Iran or Iraq major areas for bilateral Sino-Russian cooperation or significant points of confrontation with Washington.

In sum, although Chinese-Russian relations have improved along several important dimensions, security cooperation between Beijing and Moscow has remained limited, episodic, and tenuous. The two governments support each other on select issues but differ on others, as might be expected from their opportunistic relationship. Since some of their interests conflict, the relationship is not necessarily moving in a decidedly anti-American direction. Although no action undertaken by these two great powers is insignificant and Washington must continue to monitor carefully developments in Beijing and Moscow, thus far their fitfully improving ties have not presented a major security challenge to the United States or its allies.

Nevertheless, prudent U.S. national security planners should prepare for possible major discontinuities in Sino-Russian relations. American officials should employ a mixture of "shaping and hedging" policies that aim to avert a hostile Chinese-Russian alignment while concurrently preparing the United States to better counter such a development should it arise.

CHINA-RUSSIA SECURITY RELATIONS: STRATEGIC PARALLELISM WITHOUT PARTNERSHIP OR PASSION?

INTRODUCTION

American security and defense planners are increasingly concerned about the military capabilities of China and Russia. In his annual assessment of global threats to the United States issued in early February 2008, Director of National Intelligence Michael McConnell singled out the two countries as now having the technical capabilities "to target and disrupt" elements of the U.S. information and intelligence collection infrastructure.[1]

At the same time, General T. Michael Moseley, the Air Force Chief of Staff, cautioned in a speech at Air University that the United States had to plan to counter such "ascendant powers," even while improving its response to the recently prominent threats of terrorism and insurgencies.[2] The new Air Force strategic plan states: "Ascendant powers—flush with new wealth and hungry for resources and status—are posturing to contest U.S. superiority. These adaptive competitors are translating lessons from recent conflicts into new warfighting concepts and doctrines specifically designed to counter U.S. strengths and exploit vulnerabilities."[3] Moseley added that, even if it was unlikely that the U.S. military would engage in a direct conflict with China and/or Russia, "there's a 100 percent probability we will have to fight their equipment" because the two countries now sell their advanced warplanes and air defense systems throughout the world.

Meanwhile, senior commanders of the U.S. Navy have expressed concern about China's recent acquisition of advanced "area-denial weapons" such as the conventional submarines, advanced destroyers, and antiship missiles the Chinese military has purchased from Russia during the past decade. These include a dozen advanced *Kilo*-class ultra-quiet diesel submarines. Such weapons, which the Chinese now often produce themselves with Russian technical assistance, could pose a serious threat to any U.S. Navy ships that attempted to defend Taiwan from an attack by the Chinese People's Liberation Army (PLA).[4]

The improved political and economic relationship between Beijing and Moscow since the end of the Cold War has affected a range of international security issues. China and Russia have expanded their bilateral economic and security cooperation. In addition, as discussed below, they have pursued distinct but parallel policies regarding many global and regional issues. Yet, Chinese and Russian policies regarding a range of important subjects are still largely uncoordinated and sometimes in conflict. Economic ties between China and Russia remain minimal compared to those found between most friendly countries, let alone allies. Although a stronger Chinese-Russian alliance could present greater challenges to other countries (e.g., the establishment of a joint Moscow-Beijing hegemony in Central Asia), several factors make it unlikely that the two countries will form such a bloc.

At a democracy forum at the Prague Security Studies Institute on June 5, 2007, President Bush criticized both China and Russia for their undemocratic practices. He characterized U.S. relations with each country as a mixture of both cooperation and conflict: "In the areas where we share mutual interests, we work together. In other areas, we have strong disagreements." He warned that while his administration would continue to pursue better ties with both countries, the United States would do so "without abandoning our principles or our values."[5]

Although attempting to promote democracy in China and Russia has clearly proven problematic, given the evident countertendencies of their leaders, the formula of cooperating when we can and disagreeing when we must is prudent. In addition, the U.S. Government should adopt a proactive shaping and hedging strategy that will seek to prevent the emergence of a hostile Sino-Russian alignment while simultaneously preparing the United States to better counter such an alignment should it nonetheless emerge.

BILATERAL TIES

Unlike during the Cold War, China and Russia no longer fear the possibility of a shooting war with each other, at least not in the near term. Significantly, the two countries have largely accepted their common border. Yet, tensions persist over illegal Chinese immigration into Russia, as well as the inability of Chinese authorities to halt the spillover of pollution from China into Russia. Russians worry in particular about the long-term implications of China's exploding population for Russia's demographically and economically stagnant eastern regions, a situation some Russian leaders already consider to be a major security threat.

Managing Border Issues.

Since the disintegration of the Soviet Union in the early 1990s, China and Russia have resolved the most important sources of Cold War-era tensions. For example, through lengthy direct negotiations, the two governments have largely resolved their boundary disputes, which engendered armed border clashes in the late 1960s and early 1970s. In addition, they have demilitarized their 2,640-mile shared frontier (the section to the east of the Russian-Mongolian border is 2,606 miles long; that to the west is 34 miles).[6] Russia's first president, Boris Yeltsin, made border management a priority in his administration, for understandable reasons he cited in July 1995: "China is a very important state for us. It is a neighbor, with which we share the longest border in the world and with which we are destined to live and work side by side forever."[7]

Border demilitarization talks began in November 1989. They soon split into parallel negotiations, one on reducing military forces along the Chinese-Russian frontier, the other on implementing confidence- and security-building measures in the border region. In July 1994, the Russian and Chinese defense ministers agreed to a set of practices to forestall incidents. These measures included arrangements to avert unauthorized ballistic missile launches, prevent the jamming of communications equipment, and warn ships and aircraft that might inadvertently violate national borders. In September of that year, Chinese and Russian authorities pledged not to target each other's strategic nuclear missiles. They also adopted a mutual "no first use" nuclear weapons posture (these agreements are largely symbolic; they were not accompanied by any verification or enforcement procedures, and either country can rapidly retarget its intercontinental ballistic missiles). In April 1998, China and Russia established a direct presidential hot line—China's first with another government.

Immigration Issues.

Although Russians no longer worry about a potential military clash with China over border issues, and the revival of the Russian economy in recent years under President Vladimir Putin has reassured many Russians that they will not soon fall behind their Chinese counterparts in terms of their average standard of living, they do fear that the combination of the declining native population in the Russian Far East and massive Chinese immigration into the region will lead to China's long-term peaceful occupation and de facto annexation of large parts of eastern Russia. During a July 2000 visit to the Russian Far East, Putin remarked that "if we don't take concerted action, the future local population will speak Japanese, Chinese, or Korean."[8] In December 2005, Russian Interior Minister Rashid Nurgaliev reaffirmed that illegal immigration presented a threat to the security of the Russian Far East.[9]

The stark demographic and economic contrasts along the Russian-Chinese frontier are evident to all observers. According to the 2002 Census, the entire Russian Far Eastern Federal District had a population of 6.7 million inside a territory of 6.2 million square kilometers (over one-third of the total area of the Russian Federation).[10] These figures equate to an average population density of slightly more than one person per square kilometer, making the Russian Far East one of the most sparsely populated areas in the world. The population of the Russian Far East has been rapidly declining since the dissolution of the Soviet Union, falling by over 1.5 million inhabitants since 1992, or approximately 20 percent. At present, on average 274 people leave the region each day.[11] In contrast, over 100 million Chinese live in the border provinces of Heilongjiang, Jilin, and Liaoning, resulting in a population density there some 120 times greater.[12]

The population disparity would not by itself prompt massive Chinese migration into Russia. However, other factors are at work. China's recent rapid economic growth has obscured the fact that its population still has a relatively low standard of living. Although the aggregate size of the Chinese economy is now several times larger than that of Russia, China has a billion more people. As a result, the average Chinese has a lower per capita income than the typical Russian. Furthermore, China's rapid technological/economic transformation has generated more unemployed workers in China than there are people in Russia. Despite recent improvements, the Chinese territories along the China-Russia border, the source of most Chinese immigration into Russia, have not experienced the rapid economic growth or prosperity of southeastern China. Instead, northeast China remains a "rust belt," with an economy dominated by unprofitable state-owned enterprises that, through their massive lay-offs, have aggravated the region's already high unemployment.[13]

Under these conditions, supply and demand factors combine to induce Chinese laborers to seek work in Russia, where they generally can find jobs more easily and earn higher wages than if they remained at home. Chinese workers can be found in many rural areas throughout the Russian Far East. In addition, Chinese merchants and small businessmen are visibly concentrated in urban ghettos in such large Russian cities as Irkutsk, Khabarovsk, and Vladivostok, often finding a niche in the underdeveloped retail and service sectors.[14] They typically perform jobs—especially in agriculture, forestry, construction, and small retailing—that many Russians either shun or are unwilling to relocate from other regions of the country to perform.

Initial fears that the influx of workers would lead to a Chinese ethnic onslaught were clearly exaggerated. Thus far, most Chinese traders see Russia mainly as a place to work and make money—not as a permanent home. Nevertheless, the Russian government aims to address the problem before it becomes more serious, which could well be the case if extrapolations from present trends prove accurate. The Russian authorities have sought to deal with the demographic issue through a combination of specifically tailored policies to promote economic development of the Russian Far East. They are making the region more attractive for Russian workers and their families with solution efforts aimed to enhance birthrates and to reverse Russia's overall demographic decline.

On December 20, 2006, Putin chaired a special meeting of the Russian Security Council in Moscow dedicated to addressing the social and economic problems of the Russian Far East. In his public opening remarks posted on the Kremlin website, the President said that past government action had failed to overcome the district's ominous problems.[15] These included the region's declining Russian population and the dysfunctional imbalances between its internal production and foreign economic possibilities. Putin also warned that the region's failure to develop effective economic, information, and transportation networking with the rest of Russia had resulted in its continued isolation: "All these factors pose a grave threat to our political and economic positions in Asia and the Pacific, and, without any exaggeration, to the national security of Russia as a whole."

To address this situation, Putin instructed both the federal and regional authorities to draft a comprehensive program of action for developing the Russian Far East's energy industry, public utilities, border infrastructure, and transportation, logistics, and telecommunications infrastructure. Rather than simply expect federal budgetary resources drawn from other parts of Russia to be available, Putin urged national and local officials to pursue public-private partnerships, special economic zones, and innovative tariff and tax policies, as well as other creative developmental mechanisms. The president opined that, by creating new employment opportunities, these projects would make the Russian Far East a comfortable and attractive place to live, thereby helping reverse the region's demographic crisis.

Putin acknowledged that widespread organized crime and corruption continued to plague the region, aggravated by the existing immigration situation. Since the Russian government enforces strict limits on the number of visas issued to foreigners, even Chinese sources acknowledge that most Chinese working in the Far East do so illegally.[16] Their irregular status makes them vulnerable to extortion and blackmail from corrupt Russian officials such as the local police. In addition, they often become targets of Russian criminal gangs, whose members know that their Chinese victims avoid turning to Russian law enforcement agencies for protection. Furthermore, some Russians provide illegal immigration and protection service to Chinese citizens seeking to work in Russia. Finally, Chinese engaged in business activities in Russia without the proper visas typically do not pay taxes on their illegal earnings.[17]

Allowing more Chinese to enter Russia legally could help overcome these problems by reducing opportunities for profitable criminal activities. More Chinese workers and retailers would also provide additional services to the region's Russian inhabitants as well as increase price competition among the Chinese providing services. Nevertheless, until now such proposals have encountered insurmountable opposition. Many Russians fear that the increased competition from Chinese laborers and retailers would hurt the employment prospects of the native Russian community. Russian trade unions in the Far East have already complained that Chinese migrant workers are taking jobs that should go to ethnic Russians.[18] Other Russians oppose allowing more Chinese to reside in Russia on racial grounds. Most importantly, national security considerations have long made Russian government officials reluctant to relax their controls on Chinese immigration into Russia.

Instead, Putin called on federal and regional authorities to adopt urgent measures to improve the performance of the law enforcement agencies operating in the district. He cited the effectiveness of Operation ENERGY in neighboring Siberia as a model for emulation. According to Putin, the operation had led to the apprehension of many criminals and the confiscation of large sums of money that accrued to the state. In contrast, in a February 2007 visit to Vladivostok, Russian Prosecutor General Yuri Chaika chastised local law enforcement officials for failing to solve half the crimes in the region in 2006. He also complained that at least 60 major criminal groups still operated in the Vladivostok region, and that corruption still pervaded local government organizations.[19]

At the end of his opening remarks, Putin assigned to the attendees the task of establishing a government commission on the socio-economic development of the Far Eastern Federal District. The Security Council duly created a State Commission for the Development of the Far East under the chairmanship of then Prime Minister Mikhail Fradkov, with several other ministers as members.[20] Putin's presidential envoy to the region, Kamil Iskhakov, said the commission could function as a de facto federal government ministry for the Russian Far East.[21]

When he visited Vladivostok on January 27, 2007, Putin indicated that the government might spend an additional 100 billion rubles ($3.8 billion) to construct a resort and associated infrastructure on the nearby Russky Island, which would host the 2012 Asian Pacific Economic Cooperation (APEC) summit.[22] The following month, Fradkov said that the envisaged spending program would help stimulate economic growth throughout the Russian Far East in such sectors as energy, transport, and shipbuilding.[23] During his visit to the September 2007 APEC summit in Sydney, Konstantin Kosachyov, head of the Russian parliament's international affairs committee, said that the Russian government wanted to entice the country's Asian neighbors into supplying financial and technical assistance to the Russian Far East, "without which, the development of Russia as a whole is impossible."[24] Despite such brave rhetoric, however, Prime Minister Viktor Zubkov acknowledged in December 2007 that the government's plans for developing the Russian Far East remained underfunded and behind schedule.[25]

Solving the demographic problems of the Russian Far East will clearly require action to reverse the overall decline in the ethnic population of the Russian Federation. In his May 2006 annual address to the Russian Federal Assembly, Putin called Russia's demographic challenge the country's most critical national security threat.[26] From 1992 to early 2005, the population of the Russian Federation fell from 148.3 million to 143.5 million. This decline would have been even more severe if it had not been for the 6 million immigrants—many of them ethnic Russians who unwillingly found themselves inside the other newly independent Soviet republics after the Union of Soviet Socialist Republic's (USSR) unexpected dissolution—who moved back to Russian territory during this period. The Russian Statistics Service estimates that without further immigration, Russia's working age population could decline by 18-19 million during the 2005-25 period, equivalent to almost 30 percent of the current 67 million economically active Russian citizens. In October 2007, the Russian government adopted new measures to raise birthrates, lower the national mortality rate, improve public health care, and make national immigration policies more effective. Even if the Russian government immediately succeeded in raising the country's low birthrate, however, the workforce would not benefit from these new young workers until after 2025.[27]

Although the Russian economy at large is facing a shortage of low-skilled, low-paid workers, the Russian government has preferred to rely on immigration by ethnic Russians from other parts of the former Soviet Union to help fill this gap rather than encourage Chinese or other non-Slavic ethnics to immigrate to Russia. In October 2006, Putin announced that the Russian government would spend $170 million in 2007 to facilitate the voluntary repatriation of Russians living outside the Russian Federation (estimated to number 20-30 million people, with two-thirds in other former Soviet republics) to help compensate for the present 700,000 annual decline in Russia's population.[28] The authorities also allow citizens from the other former Soviet republics to work in Russia for a few years without having to obtain Russian citizenship. Thus far, however, similar initiatives adopted earlier to encourage more ethnic Russians to return to Russia have yielded far fewer returnees than desired.[29]

People from other countries, especially from the former Soviet republics but also from China, have moved to fill this vacuum. The Federal Migration Services estimate that over 10 million foreign workers enter Russia each year.[30] The Russian authorities have taken several steps to curb their commercial activities. In October 2006, Putin directed the government to establish quotas for foreign workers in Russia and limit the length of visas then permitting non-citizens to work in Russia up to 90 days during any 6-month period.[31] Starting on April 1, 2007, moreover, the government forbade foreigners from selling goods directly to Russian citizens in retail marketplaces in Russia. Non-Russian citizens legally working in Russia must restrict their retail activities to service functions such as cleaning, loading, and managing these operations.[32] To strengthen enforcement, the government increased the fines imposed on businesses employing illegal immigrants.[33]

Although these measures are primarily aimed against emigrants from Central Asia, they also affect those from China, often to the detriment of the Russian economy. These restrictions on Chinese business activities have led many to return home, and have weakened Russia's integration into the ethnic Chinese commercial networks that support economic activities in much of East Asia.[34]

One reason the authorities have cracked down on non-Russian commercial activities is as a response to a series of violent attacks against non-slavic foreigners in

Russia in recent years. Russian racists have occasionally killed ethnic Chinese as well as, more frequently, people from Central Asia and the Caucasus. In the fall of 2006, Putin attacked "ethnic gangs" that controlled Russia's retail marketplaces and advocated measures to help protect "the native Russian population."[35] But Putin also, in January 2007, denounced xenophobia, as well as ethnic and religious intolerance, as threats to Russians' human rights and the country's security.[36]

Many Russians fear that inviting Chinese guest workers into Russia, at least in areas neighboring China such as the Russian Far East, will compromise Moscow's control over the regions. They are well aware of how "temporary" foreign workers in Europe, the United States, and other countries tend to become permanent despite their "illegal" status. If large numbers of Chinese move into eastern Russia and retain their family ties and allegiance to their homeland, the Russian Far East could become absorbed de facto into China.

During President Hu Jintao's visit to Moscow in 2006, the Chinese and Russian governments agreed to draft a joint plan to develop Russia's eastern and China's northeastern regions. The cooperative regional investment agreement was signed by Russia's Vnesheconombank, the regional government of Krasnoyarsk Territory, and China's State Bank for Development, envisaging joint Sino-Russian efforts to promote construction, transportation, agriculture, public utilities, the service sector, and the development of natural resources.[37] If the Russian Far East continues to remain largely excluded from Russia's general economic revival or if Russia's recent growth surge weakens overall, then Russian fears about becoming a natural resource appendage of China will return, adversely affecting the long-term prospects for enduring Russian-Chinese security ties.

Border Pollution.

Russian experts fear that growing pollution in China will provide another stimulus for Chinese immigration into the Russian Far East. According to the World Bank, 16 of the world's 20 most polluted cities are in China—the air being so polluted that it causes 400,000 premature deaths every year.[38] The human and other costs of this pollution are staggering. The World Bank estimates that pollution costs China an annual 8-12 percent of its annual $1.4 trillion gross domestic product (GDP), through the impact of acid rain on crops, medical bills, lost work from illness, money spent on disaster relief following floods, and wasted resource depletion.[39] China's governmental structure lacks a powerful, over-arching national institution capable of coordinating, monitoring, and enforcing environmental legislation. Local Chinese authorities are typically judged on the basis of how well they promote economic growth rather than on how well they protect the local environment.[40]

Pollution flowing from China into Russia via waterways has become a serious problem. Russians complain about the environmental threat to Russian waterways (e.g., the Amur River) through the routine discharge of waste materials from Chinese industrial facilities. China has over 20,000 chemical plants that frequently spill hazardous substances into rivers. From the Russians' perspective, the most notorious incident occurred in November 2005, when an explosion at a PetroChina chemical complex in Jilin Province dumped approximately 100 tons of benzene into the Songhua

River.[41] Although the Chinese made unprecedented efforts to cooperate with the Russians to minimize the spill's impact, the accident disrupted the water supply of the Russian city of Khabarovsk, whose 600,000 residents were forced to use bottled water for drinking and cooking.[42]

Although representatives of the central Russian government are reluctant to risk antagonizing a close political and economic partner by over-zealous attacks on Chinese authorities for failing to crack down on such pollution problems, some local Russian officials are less reticient in condemning the Chinese for seemingly promoting their own national development at Russia's expense. Khabarovsk regional governor Viktor Ishayev did admit that 100 plants on the banks of the Songhua River in China discharge pollution which reached Russia's Amur River (referred to as the Heilong River in China). Local Russian leaders claimed that Chinese industries are skimping on pollution controls in order to sustain their low-cost competitive advantage over Russian and other foreign companies.[43]

In September 2006, Russian and Chinese officials signed a protocol on bilateral environmental cooperation to protect the rivers in their border region. At the meeting, held in Moscow, they also agreed to conclude a treaty which would establish mechanisms to compensate parties for damages arising from any pollution that might occur.[44] China and Russia have established bilateral task forces on environmental protection and on joint monitoring of the quality of the water of their shared transnational rivers.[45] On January 29, 2008, the Chinese and Russian governments signed "The Agreement between the Government of the People's Republic of China and the Government of the Russian Federation on Reasonable Utilization and Protection of Transboundary Waters." The accord defined the scope, contents, and methods of Sino-Russian cooperation for some 3,500 kilometers of waterways along their common border.[46] Despite these agreements, on January 30, the very next day, the Russian Security Council held a special session devoted to environmental threats, especially pollution and human-caused environmental disasters. Putin emphasized that Russia must defend its environmental interests at the international level, especially with respect to cross-border pollution.[47]

One reason Chinese and Russian officials consider these immigration and pollution problems security issues is that they generate animosity and distrust towards China by many Russians. A 2006 survey found that 40 percent of Russians consider China's rise as a threat to Russia. In a survey of assessments of China over the past years, the Pubic Opinion Foundation has found that the percentage of Russian respondents seeing China as a threat has increased from 18 percent in 2001 to 30 percent in 2006. Although many Russians living in the European part of the country share these concerns, the fears are greatest among the inhabitants of Siberia and the Russian Far East, where the people evidently most worry about Chinese immigration and its effects on Russia's territorial integrity. A recent survey found that 36 percent of the respondents in Siberia and 43 percent in the Russian Far East fear that China could eventually become a dangerous or hostile neighbor. Over 80 percent of the respondents in these regions oppose increasing the Chinese economic presence in Russia. Most impressively, unlike Russians living in western Russia, their co-nationals inhabiting Siberia and the Russian Far East would support the United States in a hypothetical conflict between Beijing and Washington.[48]

ENERGY SECURITY

In some respects, China and Russia should be natural energy partners. Chinese energy demand is soaring, and Russia's oil and gas deposits lie much closer to China than the more distant energy sources of Africa and the Persian Gulf. Yet, economic and political differences have kept the two countries divided over several vital issues relating to their mutual energy security, weakening prospects for an exclusive Russo-China energy bloc in Eurasia.

The Opportunity.

Energy security invariably represents an important agenda item at Russian-Chinese leadership summits. As a result of China's surging economy, China has become one of the world's largest purchasers of oil, natural gas, and nuclear technologies. The gap between China's stagnant energy production and fast-growing consumption is projected to expand even further in the next 2 decades. According to the Energy Information Administration, China's oil consumption is expected to rise to 15 billion barrels per day (b/d) by 2030 from 7.4 b/d in 2006. Similarly, natural gas consumption is projected to increase to 198 billion cubic meters (bcm) from 49 bcm over the same period.[49] Domestic resources will not be able to meet China's growing demand for energy in general, and for oil and natural gas in particular. Although China has substantial coal reserves (13 percent of the world supply), its oil (2-3 percent) and natural gas (1 percent) reserves are relatively small compared to China's aggregate demand, making them increasingly unable to satisfy demand. Moreover, despite Beijing's continued hopes for domestic exploration and new production of oil, it is unlikely to stem the tide of growing oil imports. The reserves of China's mature oil fields, including Daqing, Shengli, and Liaohe, which produce the majority of China's crude oil, are rapidly depleting. While gains in offshore production can help offset declines in onshore production, it is generally expected among international experts that China's crude output will be relatively flat over the next 2 decades.

This combination of limited indigenous energy resources and rising demand has prompted Chinese leaders to adopt a multifaceted energy strategy. Three major components of this strategy are: (1) reforming the energy sector to maximize domestic production and attract foreign direct investment; (2) diversifying the energy mix to reduce the nation's dependency on fossil fuels and contain pollution; and (3) diversifying international energy sources to restrain dependence on one or a few producing regions.

In principle, Russia should find a natural fit within this framework. It is the second-largest oil exporter after Saudi Arabia and possesses the world's largest reserves of natural gas. Many of its new and untapped oil and gas fields are situated in eastern Russia (in eastern Siberia and the Russian Far East) in locations closer to China than older fields that now provide energy primarily to consumers in Russia and Europe. In September 2007, the Russian Industry and Energy Ministry approved a plan proposed by Gazprom to invest $100 billion through 2030 to create an integrated production, transportation, and supply system involving over 200 billion cubic meters of natural gas in east Siberia and the Russian Far East.[50] In December 2007, Alexander Ananenkov, Deputy Chairman of the

Gazprom Management Committee, said that Russian natural gas sales to Asian and Pacific countries—especially China, Japan, and South Korea—from Siberia and the Russian Far East could reach 50 billion cubic meters by 2007.[51]

During Putin's March 2006 visit to Beijing, the two governments signed four energy cooperation agreements envisaging collaboration in oil, gas, electricity, and nuclear energy. Putin's entourage included the heads of Russia's major oil, gas, and electricity companies. The Beijing summit provided an opportunity for them to sign several cooperative agreements with their Chinese counterparts. In March 2007, President Hu signed several additional energy cooperation agreements with Russian energy partners worth billions of dollars on paper.[52] In April 2006, Russia began construction of a massive East Siberia-Pacific Ocean (ESPO) oil pipeline, which will cost an estimated $11.5 billion to complete.[53] According to present plans, the ESPO pipeline will include a branch linking China directly to eastern Siberia.[54] Russia will also build another large new pipeline to deliver billions of cubic meters of natural gas to East Asia each year. The 21st century could well see a profound eastward shift in the direction of Russian energy export routes as new supplies flow towards East Asia rather than Europe.

Nuclear energy represents another possible area of collaboration. At present, China's 11 operating nuclear reactors produce less than 2 percent of the country's electricity, compared with over 25 percent in Japan and approximately 75 percent in France.[55] The Chinese government aims to double this figure to 4 percent by 2020, with an aggregate capacity of 40,000 megawatts (MW).[56] Russia is a leading international supplier of civil nuclear energy technologies. In November 2007, China signed a preliminary agreement with Russia to build two more 1,000 MW nuclear reactors at its Tianwan nuclear power station. The parties expect to sign a formal contract in late 2008. Russia's Atomstroyexsport corporation has already constructed two reactors at Tianwan. Russian energy experts eventually hope to build a total of eight reactors at the site.[57]

The Challenge.

Despite the mutual interests as reflected in the flurry of bilateral energy cooperation, thus far various conflicts and suspicions have kept actual Russian energy exports to China at surprisingly low levels. For example, Russia's contribution to China's oil imports is approximately 11-12 percent, less than the proportion provided by some more distant African and Persian Gulf suppliers.[58] Most importantly, Russia's consistent delays in shipments, foot-dragging on the issue of pipeline construction, and attempts to play the Chinese, Asian, and European markets against each other have discouraged Chinese policymakers from viewing Russia as a reliable energy security partner.

Thus far, the main reason for the small volume of Russian oil and gas sold to China has been the underdeveloped transportation infrastructure connecting the two countries. The majority of crude oil (about 80 percent) exported to China from Russia is still shipped by railway through the Zabaikalsk-Manzhouli border oil reloading terminal on the Chita-Harbin-Vladivostok railroad. This line has limited capacity and is very costly. Not only is rail transport about two-and-a-half to three times as expensive for Russian oil producers as shipments by pipeline, but rail deliveries to China entail the added cost of switching carriers at the border because of the different track gauges used by the two countries.

Chinese and Russian energy experts agree that transporting oil and gas through pipelines would prove much more efficient. For many years, however, the two governments have engaged in contentious negotiations over which pipelines to build, where to build them, the schedule for their construction, and who will pay to build and maintain them. In particular, the repeated delays on the Russian side to conduct "feasibility" studies and "environmental impact" assessments have reinforced Chinese suspicions that their Russian interlocutors are using the specter of diverting more energy sales to China to enhance their negotiating leverage with Japan and Europe.

At the time of the March 2007 Hu-Putin summit, China's chief energy planner, National Development and Reform Commission Vice Chairman Zhang Guobao, complained about the Russian approach to the oil transportation issue as well as its natural gas and electricity policies:

> The Sino-Russia pipeline question is one step forward, two steps back. Today is cloudy with a chance for sun while tomorrow is sunny with a chance for clouds. One moment Russia is saying they have made a decision, the next saying that no decision has been made. . . . Even though there have been a lot of promises expressing Russia's interest in exporting natural gas to China, in truth no real progress has been made. As for Russian electricity exports . . . during all the years we've been connected together, Russia has only sent a total of 1 billion kilowatt hours of electricity to China.[59]

Another complication is that Russia's unexploited oil and gas deposits are located in remote areas with challenging geophysical characteristics (e.g., offshore or under frozen tundra). Russian companies need considerable foreign capital and technology to exploit these fields effectively and upgrade the country's aging energy transportation infrastructure.[60] Beijing wants Moscow to devote resources to construction of a fixed permanent pipeline to China as proof of Russia's commitment to a long-term supply relationship. Russians are skeptical, however, because they know that their ability to attract Western capital could decline if they actually build pipelines committing them as primary supplier of the Chinese import market. Although Russians have been discussing constructing an oil pipeline to China for over a decade, they continue to entice Japan, Europe, and even the United States with offers of future energy deliveries—encouraging them to offer financial and technical assistance as well as to moderate their policies on other contentious issues (e.g., the Japanese-Russian territorial dispute over the Kuril islands). Furthermore, despite Russian companies consolidating control over Central Asian oil and gas resources, many analysts doubt Russia's ability to satisfy all these expanding energy markets given its stagnant domestic production.

A further difficulty is that the Russian government under Putin has not exempted China from its efforts to limit foreign control of its major energy assets. According to one estimate, the share of Russian crude oil that is produced by government-controlled energy companies has risen from less than one-fifth in 2000 to almost half in 2007, with many of the remaining private firms still essentially under the Kremlin's thumb.[61] In 2002, the Russian Duma blocked China's National Petroleum Corporation (CNPC) from acquiring a majority stake in Slavneft, a key Russian oil producer, even though CNPC's bid was almost twice as high as that of the eventual domestic winner.[62] In June 2006, the Russian authorities did allow China's Sinopec to purchase a major stake in Udmurtneft, a major Russian oil producer, but only on the condition that it resold sufficient shares to give the Russian state-owned energy conglomerate Rosneft a 51 percent majority stake in the enterprise.[63] As long as Russian energy firms remain under state control, Chinese policymakers—aware of Moscow's energy confrontation with Georgia, Ukraine, and other countries whose governments have antagonized the Kremlin—must worry that relying on them for crucial energy supplies could leave Beijing vulnerable to politically motivated reductions and cut-offs.

Elements of competition and conflict exist also with respect to civil nuclear energy cooperation. The Chinese government has taken care to purchase advanced nuclear power plants from France and the United States as well as Russia. One reason for Beijing's approach is that Russian suppliers have hesitated to sell China their most advanced energy technologies. As with their weapons sales, Russians worry that Chinese scientists and technicians will learn from any transferred technology how to further improve the quality of their indigenous production. Not only would this reduce Chinese interest in purchasing Russian nuclear technology, but China could become a formidable competitor in the third-country nuclear energy markets such as Egypt, Myanmar, and perhaps even India.[64]

Another reason China refuses to purchase only Russian nuclear technologies is to remind Moscow that Beijing, too, has energy options. For years, Russian energy companies and government officials have been playing off potential foreign purchasers of its energy against each other. Threatening Europeans with the specter of diverting future Russia energy shipments to Asia, and vice versa, has been a favorite tactic. For example, in the course of his company's difficult negotiations with potential Chinese buyers of Russian oil delivered by rail through Mongolia, Sergei Bogdanchikov, the president of Rosneft, warned that "our partners must understand that Russia has a surplus rather than a deficit of pipeline capacity, and we can also supply oil to Europe. . . . So here is a market situation for you—[which side willingly] pays more?"[65] By purchasing its nuclear reactors from U.S.-based Westinghouse and France's Areva, China's officials have demonstrated that it, too, could exploit competition among the multiple U.S., European, and Asian energy suppliers eager to do business with China.

RUSSIAN MILITARY SALES TO CHINA

For over a decade, Russian military exports to China have constituted the most important dimension of the two countries' security relationship. Russian firms have derived substantial revenue from the sales, which also helped sustain Russia's military industrial complex during the lean years of the 1990s. The PLA was able to acquire advanced conventional weapons that Chinese firms could not yet manufacture. Now this situation is changing. The Chinese defense industry has become capable of producing much more sophisticated armaments. Moscow now confronts the choice of either seeing its Chinese market decrease dramatically or agreeing to sell even more advanced weapons to Beijing, knowing that the second choice could destabilize military force balances in East Asia.

Background.

Since the two governments signed an agreement on military-technical cooperation in December 1992, China has purchased more defense items from the Russian Federation than from all other countries combined. During the 1990s, the value of these deliveries ranged up to $1 billion annually. In recent years, this figure has approached $2 billion per year. According to one estimate, between 1992 and 2006, the total value of Russian arms exports to China amounted to approximately $26 billion worth of military equipment and weapons.[66] These sales helped make Russia the world's largest arms supplier to Asian countries between 1998 and 2005, well ahead of the United States.[67]

Through these dealings, the Chinese Navy and Air Force have acquired dozens of Su-27 *Flanker* fighter jets and Su-30 *Flanker* multirole aircraft; Mi-17 transport helicopters; Il-76 military transport aircraft; IL-78M *Midas* in-flight refueling tankers; A-50 warning and control aircraft; T-72 main battle tanks; Mi-8 and Mi-17 helicopters; armored personnel carriers; *Kilo*-class Project 636 diesel submarines; several *Sovremenny*-class destroyers; a variety of antiship, air defense, and other missiles; and other advanced conventional military systems or their components. Between 1998 and 2005, moreover, the Chinese manufactured over a hundred Su-27Sk warplanes under Russian license, using many Russian parts in the assembly process.[68]

Moscow's decision to sell advanced conventional weapons systems to China results primarily from economic rather than strategic considerations. Despite the recent rise in national defense spending, the Russian government resists allocating substantial financial resources to restructuring the Russian defense industry. Citing the need to avoid repeating the Soviet mistake of competing in a ruinously expensive arms race, President Vladimir Putin and other Russian leaders have reaffirmed their commitment to hold annual military expenditures below 3 percent of Russia's GDP. Instead, government officials have encouraged Russian defense enterprises to sell their products abroad to earn additional revenue for reinvestment and to keep skilled workers from moving into civilian employment.

Unlike energy—the other commercial sector where Russian exporters can compete effectively with foreign sellers—arms exports generate high-tech manufacturing employment as well as revenue. Government officials also appreciate that many Russian companies require increased investment to develop the type of advanced conventional weapons systems that have proven so effective for Western militaries in recent wars. International markets for Russian weapons systems, upgrades, maintenance, and spare parts help sustain production lines and workers that provide essential support for the Russian military. For example, foreign funding largely paid for the development of the Su-30, which has since been incorporated into the Russian air force.

There are several reasons for China's interest in acquiring Russian arms. Economic factors come into play insofar as, by purchasing Russian weapons, China avoids having to research, develop, and manufacture its own systems. Although China's indigenous arms industry has become more capable along with the rest of the economy, Chinese defense enterprises still lag behind their leading international counterparts in several key areas, such as advanced aviation and naval weapons. For its more sophisticated heavy fighters, the PLA Air Force (PLAAF) still relies on Russian-designed planes, the Su-27 and the Su-30. Russian enterprises became the dominant foreign supplier of China's advanced weapons systems after the 1989 Tiananmen Square incident led Western governments to prohibit their own companies from selling advanced military technologies to China.

The Changing Market.

Although the Russian government and its defense enterprises would like to perpetuate the existing commercial arrangement, the increasing sophistication of China's defense industry is enabling Chinese manufacturers to produce more advanced weapons systems under license instead of purchasing finished systems directly from Russian manufacturers. Russians prefer to sell off-the-shelf items, while the Chinese favor joint or licensed production arrangements that transfer Russian technology and manufacturing capabilities to China. For several years, China has been manufacturing the Su-27 under license. The PLA has shown less interest in buying complete Russian weapons platforms such as turn-key warplanes and warships. Instead, the Chinese military has been importing more defense technologies, subsystems, and other essential components that Chinese manufacturers incorporate directly into Chinese-designed weapons systems. China purchased Russian aircraft engines for its own FC-1 fighter aircraft.[69] In January 2007, the Chinese military unveiled the *Jian-10,* a home-built fighter-bomber that uses Chinese engines and Chinese missiles.[70]

Concerns about the quality of the weapons it has been purchasing from Russia have also encouraged China to seek to enhance its indigenous production capabilities. According to the Russian press, the Chinese have complained about the poor quality of some of the weapons they have received from Russia, repeatedly postponing scheduled meetings of the Russian-Chinese Commission on Military-Technical Cooperation in protest.[71]

Another looming threat could be possible competition from European defense companies if the European Union (EU) were to lift its comprehensive arms embargo on China, imposed after the violent government repression of student protests in 1989. By selling more advanced weapons to China now, Russia would help lock in future sales and raise the barrier to entry for potential EU competitors, who would find it difficult to match Russia's low-price advantage but might prove competitive in terms of quality (EU competitors might also benefit from a Chinese desire to reward the EU for changing its embargo policy towards China).

Moscow's Choice.

The ongoing improvement in the quality of China's national defense production and the ever-present threat of additional foreign competition confront Russian officials with a difficult choice. Until now, the Russian government has refused to sell its most advanced weapons systems—such as long-range strategic bombers or ballistic missiles—to China for fear that such weapons could disrupt the balance of power in East Asia. This policy has meant that Moscow's arms sales to Beijing have not been sufficient by themselves to enable China to defeat the more technologically advanced militaries of Taiwan or Japan. But Chinese firms should soon be able to substitute their own technologies for many of the expensive defense items the PLA has acquired from Russian suppliers in the past.

These developments have resulted in Russia's arms exports to China declining from 40 percent of all sales in 2006 to less than 20 percent in 2007.[72] Partly as a result, Russia's annual bilateral trade level has gone from a multibillion dollar surplus in 2006 to a multibillion deficit last year.[73]

In order to restore its former share of China's defense market, the Russian government might decide to sell even more advanced weapons systems to Beijing. On August 26, 2005, a "high-ranking source in the Russian Defense Ministry" told the Russian news agency Interfax-AVN that Russia had deliberately showcased its Tu-95MS and the Tu-22M3 at the bilateral August "Peace Mission 2005" exercises to entice Chinese buyers. Although these strategic bombers are older platforms (the Tu-160 is Russia's most advanced strategic bomber), they can launch long-range cruise missiles against air and ground targets, including U.S. aircraft carriers.[74] The sales motive was also evident in the Russian decision to leave the bombers that participated in the exercise, as well as other types of military aircraft, on display in China for several days. The policy of exploiting the opportunity to highlight a few advanced weapons systems to the Chinese during the exercise may have worked, since Beijing placed a large order for one of the participating warplanes, the Il-78 tanker, a few weeks later.[75]

Another possible post-Soviet export item might include some advanced weapons that Russian defense systems are beginning to produce. More than 50 Russian defense companies displayed their wares at the Sixth

China International Aviation and Aerospace Exhibition held in October-November 2006 in Zhuhai in southern China.[76] For example, Moscow could approve the sale of its fourth-generation diesel-electric (*Lada* class) submarines, which would increase China's military potential against the United States and its Pacific allies. According to the Stockholm International Peace Research Institute (SIPRI), the Russian government has already offered to sell China Su-33 and Su-35 advanced combat aircraft, which are still under development.[77]

A senior Russian defense official, Alexander Denisov, once even said that Russia was prepared to assist China to design an aircraft carrier. Denisov stated to members of the news media, "Such a request would not contradict any international agreements or rules."[78] Moreover, the Russian news media have carried reports of alleged Russian assistance in helping China develop a carrier fleet. For example, there have been claims that Rosoboronexport has been negotiating a massive deal to sell China about 50 Su-33 Naval *Flanker* sea-based fighter aircraft. The estimated $2.5 billion price tag would represent "the second most expensive national arms sales contract after a $3 billion agreement for the assembly of 140 Su-MKI fighters in India under a Russian license."[79]

Selling even more advanced weapons to China could undermine Russian interests in ways that, on balance, might exceed the benefits Moscow might accrue from the arms sales. First, the governments of Taiwan, the United States, and possibly Japan and other countries would criticize the sales as destabilizing. In enhancing China's air and maritime power projection capabilities, Russian officials would be increasing the risk of military adventurism by Beijing. With more advanced warplanes and warships, the war option would look better to China. Taiwan, Japan, Vietnam, and other countries that presently have territorial disputes with China might hold Moscow responsible for the increased risks of war.

In addition, a substantial factor weighing against a Russian decision to transfer even more advanced military systems is that Chinese engineers might learn enough from the technology to further improve the quality of their indigenous production. Russian and other analysts cite past instances of Chinese technicians copying Russian weapons systems and, after making slight adjustments in their specifications (e.g., changing the caliber of an antimissile system from 100 to 105 millimeters), selling them for export.[80]

The expanding capabilities of the Chinese defense industry became evident in November 2006 when the Aviation Industries of China displayed a new air-launched supersonic cruise missile at the Sixth China International Aviation and Aerospace Exhibition held in Zhuhai. The ramjet-powered missile will allow the PLA Navy (PLAN) to attack U.S. aircraft carriers and other ships within a 400 km radius. For its antiship cruise missiles, China has until now relied on such Russian imports as the SS-N-22 *Sunburn* and SS-N-27B *Sizzler*.[81] Russian defense firms have already confronted increasingly unwelcome Chinese competition in third-country arms markets, such as in Egypt and Myanmar. In some developing countries that previously bought predominantly Soviet arms, Russian firms have yielded much of the market to lower-cost Chinese suppliers. If China is finally able to develop advanced indigenous weapons systems for export—like the long-awaited J-10 multipurpose fighter plane—China could become an even more formidable competitor.

Russian officials faced a stark choice in 2006 and 2007 when Chinese companies requested of Beijing that it grant them a license to deliver at least 150 FC-1 *Fierce Dragon* fighter planes, equipped with Russian RD-93 engines, to Pakistan. China had previously signed an end-user agreement that requires Russian government approval before China can reexport the RD-93 engine to a third country. Chinese and Pakistani firms are jointly developing the FC-1, which is known as the JF-17 *Thunder* fighter in Pakistan. On the one hand, refusing the Chinese reexport request would have made Beijing more reluctant to purchase Russian technology in the future. On the other hand, granting the reexport license in the case of the FC-1 would—besides antagonizing India, Russia's second leading arms purchaser after China—make it harder to deny similar Chinese requests to sell the planes to other countries. Chinese manufacturers hope that foreign sales of the FC-1 (a single-engine delta-winged fighter manufactured primarily at the Chengdu Aeronautical Complex) will help transform China into a leading seller of advanced combat aircraft to developing countries, many of which currently purchase Russian military aircraft.[82]

According to the Russian news media, in April 2007, President Putin personally gave China permission to reexport the Russian RD-93 engines to Pakistan as a one-time arrangement. The Ministry of Defense, Rosoboronexport, and other key actors in the Russian military-industrial complex supported granting the waiver to ensure that China would stick with its agreement to buy the engines. Under the terms of a 2005 contract, China will pay Russian suppliers $238 million for the purchase of 100 RD-93 engines as well as the associated spare parts and maintenance. China is also considering purchasing as many as 1,000 engines if the Russian suppliers upgrade their capabilities.[83] The Pakistani Air Force received its first two JF-17 aircraft in December 2007.[84] The following month, the plane entered into mass assembly, combining parts from China and Pakistan with the Russian engines, in a plant in northwest Pakistan.[85]

An even more worrisome possibility would be China's employment of Russian defense technologies in a future war with Taiwan, India, the United States, or even with Russia itself. Some Russians fear that a peaceful acquisition or military conquest of Taiwan by China would allow Beijing to redirect any further expansionist ambitions against Russia's Central Asian allies or the underpopulated Russian Far East.[86] Although a possible Sino-Russian military conflict presently seems remote, some of the weapons systems China is acquiring from Russia could remain operational for decades. Russians should recall that during the Sino-Soviet border clashes of the late 1960s, the Chinese forces employed Soviet-supplied weapons against their former patrons.

Finally, Russia's progress in selling arms to other countries might render moot Moscow's temptation to sell more powerful weapons to China, particularly in view of the fear of some Russian strategists that Beijing might one day present a "major threat" to Russia.[87] In recent years, the Russian government and its defense companies have negotiated major arms sales deals with Algeria, India, Indonesia, Venezuela, and other countries. As noted, Russia's military exports to China in 2007 declined to around 20 percent from 40 percent of its total military exports to all countries. Most of this decrease resulted from a reduction in Chinese purchases, but other countries have been increasing their own purchases. In any case, Chinese clients will still need to buy spare parts and upgrades for the Russian weapons systems they have been acquiring in such large numbers in recent years.

OTHER MILITARY COOPERATION

China and Russia participate in other forms of military cooperation in addition to their arms trade. The two armed forces regularly engage in exchanges of military officers. Frequent visits take place between senior military officials, including annual meetings of defense ministers and the chiefs of staffs of the armed forces of both countries. In March 2006, for instance, PLA Chief of Staff General Liang Guanglie met with the Russian Chief of Staff, the Russian Defense Minister, and the Russian Security Council in Moscow, reciprocating a visit by the Russian Chief of Staff to Beijing the previous March.[88] Contacts take place even more often among mid-level military officers, especially those in charge of border security units. Exchanges between military units in neighboring Chinese and Russian territories have become more frequent as well.

In August 18-25, 2005, the two countries engaged in an unprecedented bilateral military exercise, Peace Mission 2005, with the first phase in the Russian Far East and the second in China's Shandong province. Although their nominal focus was on combating terrorism and restoring peace among hypothetical local hostiles, the exercises involved large-scale air, sea, and ground operations, including Chinese submarines, Russian strategic bombers, and 8,000 and 2,000 troops from China and Russia, respectively. The maneuvers included neutralizing antiaircraft defenses, enforcing a maritime blockade, and various amphibious and maritime operations. Not even during the 1950s, when

China was a member of the Soviet bloc and a party to a formal mutual defense treaty with Moscow, had the two countries carried out such a large joint exercise.

Nevertheless, the level of interoperability was not extensive. Although the two militaries operated in the same location and time frame, they did not rehearse combined operations in the manner of the U.S. military and its military allies.[89] Although the current friendship treaty prohibits either country from joining "any alliance or bloc which damages the sovereignty, security, and territorial integrity of the other party," it provides only for consultations in the case of mutual threats, and lacks a mutual defense clause.

The joint exercises may have had several other objectives. For both countries, the large-scale maneuvers demonstrated their military capabilities. For China's military, growing in both size and sophistication, it was also an opportunity to practice operational procedures and coordination of large and varied forces. For Russia, if it considers that China may one day become a threat, it was a chance to gauge the capability of the potential enemy's military. Finally, since China is the largest purchaser of Russian weapons, the exercises offered an opportunity to conduct arms business as well as strategic maneuvers. During the exercises, Russia showed off its Tu-95 strategic bombers and Tu-22M long-range bombers. Indeed, Peace Mission 2005 could be seen as an elaborate stage for the demonstration of Russian military technology to potential Chinese buyers. Subsequent exercises have been held under Shanghai Cooperation Organization (SCO) auspices or, as in the case of the September "Cooperation 2007" bilateral drill involving Russia's interior forces and the Chinese People's Armed Police (PAP), under less elaborate ad hoc arrangements.

Global Security Issues.

In public, Beijing and Moscow are the best of friends, professing to share a comprehensive vision of how they want the world to evolve over the next few years. Their joint statements call for a multipolar world in which the United Nations (UN) and international law dominate decision making on all important questions, including the possible use of force by its members. They also stress traditional interpretations of national sovereignty rather than the application of universal democratic values. Yet, they continue to differ on important global issues, including ballistic missile defense (BMD) and military operations in space.

Mutually Supportive Policy Statements.

During the past decade, Chinese and Russian officials have issued numerous joint statements—most notably their 2001 Treaty of Good-Neighborly and Friendly Cooperation—affirming their commitment to enhanced bilateral cooperation. When Chinese President Hu Jintao visited Russia in March 2007, he set forth five principles to govern development of the "China-Russia strategic partnership" during the next decade: (1) develop bilateral political ties and enhance mutual support on issues of vital importance to either side; (2) continue to strengthen mutually profitable economic and commercial ties; (3) establish a scientific and technological partnership at multiple levels; (4) promote humanitarian cooperation in such areas as culture, health care, tourism, and other social dimensions; and (5) strengthen their cooperation on peace and security issues, both bilaterally and within multilateral institutions such as the SCO.[90]

An important feature of these joint declarations is that they also aim to influence the thinking of third parties. Chinese and Russian leaders appreciate that their combined statements resonate louder than the pronouncements of each government speaking unilaterally. For example, the joint declaration issued at the end of the March 2007 Hu-Putin summit states: "The shared position on major international political issues of principle and the common or similar positions on important international and regional issues between China and Russia enable them to take part in international cooperation more effectively and meet new challenges and threats. The two sides will continue coordination and deepen strategic coordination in diplomatic affairs to create an enabling international environment for the development of the two countries."[91]

Chinese-Russian joint statements regularly affirm their shared commitment to upholding traditional interpretations of national sovereignty, which severely limit the right of external actors to challenge a state's internal policies. In general, they reject the principle that all states must conform to any universal political or economic standards. In particular, they have expressed concern about the Bush administration's democracy promotion agenda, which they believe has contributed to the "color revolutions" that deposed the incumbent authoritarian governments in Georgia, Ukraine, and Kyrgyzstan. Instead, Chinese and Russian leaders regularly call on the international community to respect the peculiar historical political traditions of each nation and insist on the right of each country to choose its own economic and political development path.

Although these declarations do not typically refer to the United States explicitly, the target of their criticisms is obvious. In place of an American-dominated international system, the two governments frequently call for a "multipolar" world—one that "will promote multilateralism and democracy in international relations."[92] In such a framework, Russia and China would occupy key positions and no one great power (i.e., the United States) would predominate.

Beijing and Moscow frequently express a desire to strengthen the role of the United Nations in international security. As permanent members of the UN Security Council (UNSC), they can use their right to veto actions to prevent the United States and its allies from obtaining formal UN endorsement of any military operations they oppose. For this reason, the U.S. decision to lead military interventions in the former Yugoslavia and in Iraq without explicit UNSC approval evoked dismay in both capitals.[93] The two, but especially Russia, registered vociferous objections to Kosovo's declaration of independence from Serbia without the formal approval of the UNSC.[94]

Chinese and Russian officials generally oppose the use of threats to employ force or sanctions to induce other governments to change their internal or external behavior. Chinese and Russian officials have led the opposition against imposing rigorous sanctions on Iran, North Korea, and other countries that have pursued policies that Western governments consider violations of international laws and norms. The fact that both countries—in particular, their government agencies and nominally independent private defense trading companies—have been sanctioned on numerous occasions by the United States and its allies has likely contributed to their distaste for such measures.

In January 2007, the two governments cast their first parallel vetoes in the UNSC against a U.S.-sponsored resolution censoring Myanmar's authoritarian government. Russian Ambassador to the UN Vitaly I. Churkin argued that the situation in Burma did not fall within the Security Council's purview since it did not represent an immediate threat to international peace. Chinese Ambassador Wang Guangya observed simply that "no country is perfect. Similar problems exist in other countries as well."[95]

As a general rule, Chinese and Russian officials also avoid criticizing each other's domestic policies. Russian representatives have not challenged the Chinese government's repression of civil liberties and have not supported American-backed efforts to censure China's internal policies. They also have not refrained from selling military technologies that the Chinese military and police could use to repress domestic opposition. Chinese officials have reciprocated by not joining Western criticisms of Putin's authoritarian tendencies or Russia's harsh policies in Chechnya.

The reluctance of the two governments to criticize one another was evident during the recent controversy surrounding China's January 2007 test of an anti-satellite (ASAT) weapon. In contrast to the position taken by most of the world's leaders, Russian officials refused to criticize China for conducting the first test of an ASAT weapon in space in over 2 decades, ending an informal global moratorium on such actions. A week after the January 12th test, an unnamed official from the Russian Ministry of Defense told the news media that the Chinese test "was a consequence of extremely aggressive U.S. policies" that had undermined international law and led to "a new arms race in which Russia has no intention of taking part."[96]

Similarly, when a reporter subsequently asked Putin about the test during his late January 2007 visit to India, he responded by criticizing U.S. plans for space-based weapons, which he claimed had provoked the Chinese ASAT weapon test. At the January 25th press conference, Putin, alluding to earlier American and Soviet ASAT programs, remarked that China was not the first country to conduct such a test. After observing that "we should not let this genie out of the bottle," Putin reaffirmed Russian support for negotiating an agreement banning all weapons from outer space.[97] The following month, the Chinese and Russian delegations resumed their joint effort to induce the Conference on Disarmament in Geneva to adopt a treaty banning weapons in outer space, while condemning the United States for single-handedly blocking progress on this measure.[98]

Limited Missile Defense Cooperation.

Both the Chinese and Russian governments have expressed concern about the efforts of the United States and its allies to strengthen their BMD capabilities. Their professed fear is that these strategic defense systems, in combination with the strong American offensive nuclear capabilities, might enable the United States to obtain nuclear superiority over China and Russia, as propounded in a widely cited *Foreign Affairs* article by Keir Lieber and Daryl Press.[99] Former Russian Prime Minister Igor Gaidar claimed that the article, which the authors enlarged upon in a subsequent article in *International Security,* sounded almost like a deliberate "provocation" designed to induce Russia and China to collaborate on nuclear and ballistic missile technology.[100]

Russian government representatives have been most vocal in expressing their concerns about U.S. BMD plans. In July 2006, General Yury Baluyevskiy, Chief of the Russian General Staff and First Deputy Defense Minister, published a comprehensive critique of U.S. BMD plans in Russia's leading defense weekly, *Voenno-Promishlenniy Kur'er*.[101] Since then, senior Russian government officials, military officers, and policy analysts have waged a year-long campaign of invective against American foreign and defense policies, with many of their objections focusing on the U.S. proposals to deploy BMD interceptor missiles in Poland and an advanced BMD radar system in the Czech Republic.

The central Russian argument is that the professed U.S. justification for the deployments—that the systems are needed to defend the United States and European countries against a growing missile threat from would-be proliferating states—especially Iran—lacks credibility. Russian representatives further argue that the best means to discourage any aspirations these states might have in this regard is through negotiations aimed at addressing their underlying security concerns rather than through military means likely to trigger a threatening counter-response.

Given their skepticism regarding the need to erect missile defenses against Iran, Russian representatives have argued that other considerations explain U.S. interest in enhancing its missile defenses. Some Russian commentators attribute Washington's BMD plans to the machinations of the American military-industrial complex or a U.S. desire to reassert influence in Europe following the Iraq debacle. Most Russian analysts, however, see the planned BMD deployments in Poland and the Czech Republic as aimed primarily at weakening Russia's nuclear deterrent.

Preoccupation with Russia's resistance to the proposed U.S. deployments in Europe has obscured Russian opposition to other U.S. BMD programs. In his February 2007 speech at the Munich security conference, Putin indicated that Moscow saw the European deployments as one component of a larger American effort to negate Russia's nuclear deterrent and reinforce Washington's global influence. According to him, if the United States effectuates its missile defense plans, "The balance of powers will be absolutely destroyed, and one of the parties will benefit from the feeling of complete security. This means that its hands will be free not only in local but eventually also in global conflicts."[102]

Russian defense experts acknowledge that Russia's vast strategic missile arsenal could undoubtedly overwhelm the small number of interceptor missiles—currently 10—that the United States plans to deploy in Poland. They claim, however, that the United States could easily deploy additional BMD systems, including more interceptor missiles, in Poland in the future. Russian analysts have also expressed concerns that American statements regarding the evolving nature of the U.S. global BMD architecture mean the United States will seek to deploy BMD systems in other countries besides Poland and the Czech Republic, especially Ukraine or Georgia.[103] In addition, some Russian experts argue that the United States is seeking the capacity to rapidly replace the defensive interceptors with offensive ballistic missiles that could attack Russia with little warning time.[104] Russian analysts also assert that the United States will use the pretext of defending the BMD assets to deploy additional military infrastructure, including U.S. ground and air forces, close to Russia, despite alleged promises made at the time of Germany's reunification that North

Atlantic Treaty Organization (NATO) governments would refrain from such forward deployments.

Accompanying each of these discrete criticisms has been the expression of a general Russian grievance that the BMD dialogue U.S. officials have offered Moscow has been insufficiently comprehensive or detailed. Russians complain that these bilateral briefings have essentially consisted of a review of U.S. plans, with assurances that their implementation would not threaten Russia, rather than a genuine exchange of views in which Americans take into account Russian concerns.[105] Some Russians have accused the Bush administration of feigning an effort at consultation with Moscow to appease Europeans worried about possible Russian countermeasures.[106]

Russian government officials and military commanders have actively sought to exacerbate these concerns. During the past year, Putin and other Russian leaders have stressed their country's development of advanced military technologies that will guarantee Russia's ability to overcome any U.S. or NATO BMD systems. On May 29, 2007, the Russian government ostentatiously tested two new ballistic missiles, designated the RS-24 and R-500. First Deputy Prime Minister Sergei Ivanov, the former Defense Minster, claimed that "these systems can beat any operational and future missile defenses."[107] Russian military commanders have repeatedly warned that they will target any U.S. BMD sites near Russia with Russian ballistic missiles or warplanes.[108] Putin and other Russian leaders have renounced any intent to match the U.S. military buildup on a missile-for-missile basis, expressing confidence that less costly asymmetric responses would adequately maintain the credibility of Russia's nuclear deterrent. Nonetheless, they still want to underscore to domestic and foreign audiences that Russia retains a formidable strategic arsenal.

Moscow's initial response—vociferous complaints punctuated by vague threats of retaliation—failed to induce either Washington or its enthusiastic NATO allies to cancel the BMD programs. Russian representatives then pursued several diplomatic initiatives to avert the deployments. At the 2007 G-8 summit, Putin offered to provide the United States with unprecedented access to data on Iranian nuclear developments as gleaned from the Russian-leased Gabala radar station in Azerbaijan in return for a freeze of Washington's planned Czech and Polish deployments. At their July 2-3 Kennebunkport summit, Putin told Bush that the United States could also use a nearly-constructed BMD radar in southern Russia, located in Krasnodar Territory about 700 km northwest of Iran. Putin further proposed establishing an ambitious pan-European BMD architecture that would integrate NATO and Russian defenses against common missile threats. The Bush administration, while expressing general interest in expanding BMD cooperation with Moscow, refused to accept Putin's specific offers because they would have required abandoning the planned U.S. missile defenses in Eastern Europe. Even if a future U.S. administration seems more amenable to such a deal, the prospects for extensive Russian-American BMD cooperation are unpromising. Fundamentally, multinational missile defense arrangements demand an exceptional level of military-to-military cooperation between participating countries, which in turn generally requires good political relations among the governments. Russia and the United States have proven unable to achieve the requisite improvement in their bilateral relationship and seem unlikely to do so in the near future.[109]

The Chinese have also criticized U.S. BMD plans, if somewhat less vocally than their Russian counterparts, and have expressed no formal interest in collaborating with the United States on missile defense. China's state-run news media have generally supported the Russian criticisms of U.S. BMD programs.[110] Chinese officials have focused their attention on the expanding U.S.-Japanese BMD research and development program. A particular Chinese concern has been that the system might eventually cover Taiwan, a development which could embolden Taiwanese separatists if it appeared to negate the capacity of China's growing fleet of medium-range missiles to bombard the island.[111] Some commentators have interpreted China's January 2007 ASAT test and the expected deployment of China's new DF-31 road-mobile intercontinental ballistic missile as efforts to enhance China's ability to overcome any BMD deployed by the United States or its East Asian allies.[112]

Despite their mutual concern about American strategic ambitions, however, Russia and China have not undertaken any widespread collaboration in this area. For example, they have not pooled their military resources or expertise to counter U.S. BMD technologies. Nor have they coordinated pressures against other countries in Europe or Asia to abstain from deploying U.S. BMD assets, even in Central Asia or Northeast Asia, regions which border both their territories.

Both Russia and China have worked in the UNSC to weaken resolutions seeking to sanction Iran for activities that NATO leaders claim might provide Tehran with nuclear weapons or long-range ballistic missiles. Even so, Russian and Chinese representatives have thus far limited their collaboration on the missile defense issue to joint declarations. It was not until July 19, 2007, that the Chinese Foreign Ministry also endorsed Russia's position against U.S. plans to deploy BMD systems in Poland and the Czech Republic, agreeing that it could upset the global balance of power. Chinese Foreign Ministry spokesperson Liu Jianchao stated that "China always holds that the deployment of an anti-ballistic missile system will undermine the current international strategic balance and stability. It is not conducive to regional security and mutual trust between countries, and might give rise to new problems of missile proliferation and end up with an arms race." [113]

Russian officials have also expressed disapproval of Japanese and Australian participation in U.S. BMD programs.[114] But they have not devoted anywhere near as much attention to this dimension as they have to the planned U.S. BMD deployments in Eastern Europe, which many Russian strategists consider a special security zone given its proximity to Moscow, St. Petersburg, and Russia's European industrial heartland.

At the August 2007 SCO summit, Russian Foreign Minister Sergey Lavrov stated that Russia and China were "analyzing the U.S. global missile defense plans targeting Europe and the East," but explained that both governments were addressing the issue independently, though in parallel, and had not yet considered formally cooperating on BMD. Such collaboration could presumably range from simply exchanging intelligence assessments to establishing bilateral research and development programs for producing joint anti-BMD technologies. Lavrov would state only that Beijing and Moscow "share a vision of how to provide security."[115]

Space-Based Suspicions.

As in other areas, China and Russia have both parallel and conflicting interests in outer space. The two countries have long cooperated on civilian space research missions. Many of China's space exploration capabilities are based on former Soviet technologies. China and Russia still conduct joint research missions. For example, the two countries intend to launch two jointly developed and manufactured exploration craft to Mars next year. One of the twin explorers, under the control of China's National Space Administration, will orbit the planet. The other, guided by Russia's Space Agency (RosKosmos), will land on the planet.[116]

Both governments have long been concerned by U.S. military programs in this realm. For example, when the Bush administration published an unclassified version of its new National Space Policy in October 2006, it evoked deep concern in Moscow and Beijing. Although it acknowledges the value of international cooperation in space and the right of "free passage" for all countries' satellites and other space-based objects, the policy reaffirms the intent to protect U.S. space capabilities by all available means.[117]

The 1967 Outer Space Treaty prohibits countries from basing weapons of mass destruction (WMD) in space, but its application to space-based missile defenses involving lasers or other non-nuclear weapons remains under dispute. Russian and Chinese experts claim that the United States is seeking to acquire the means to orchestrate attacks in space against Russian and Chinese reconnaissance satellites and long-range ballistic missiles, whose trajectories pass through the upper atmosphere.[118] Accordingly, Chinese and Russian delegations to various UN disarmament meetings have submitted joint working papers and other proposals to begin multilateral disarmament negotiations to prevent the militarization of space. The U.S. Government opposes a formal arms control treaty for space as both unnecessary and probably ineffective.[119]

In addition to these diplomatic initiatives, the Russian and Chinese governments have independently issued broad threats intended to dissuade the United States from actually deploying (as opposed to merely researching) weapons in space. For instance, in June 2005 Russian Defense Minister Sergei Ivanov threatened "adequate retaliatory measures" against any country that deployed spaced-based weapons.[120] After the new U.S. space policy was first announced in September 2006, Vladimir Popovkin, the commander of Russian Space Forces, said Russia "must be ready to take adequate offensive and defensive measures" if other countries were to develop and deploy space-based weapons.[121] Vitaly Davydov, the deputy head of the Russian space agency RosKosmos, complained that the U.S. October 2006 National Space policy document "can be seen today as the first step toward a serious deepening of the military confrontation in space. Now the Americans are saying that they want . . . to dictate to others who else is allowed to go there."[122]

As noted, the Russian government used the occasion of China's anti-satellite test on January 12, 2007, to criticize the United States for blocking progress on outer space arms control negotiations. The Russian reaction was unusually restrained, given that China's decision to conduct its first test of an ASAT weapon represents a sharp escalation in the hitherto low-key positioning between China, Russia, and the United States over the use of outer space for military purposes. The test represented the first anti-satellite attempt by any country in over 2 decades. It also marked the first use of a surface-based missile to destroy an orbiting satellite.

Nevertheless, the Chinese and Russian delegations continued to work at the UN Conference on Disarmament in Geneva to secure enactment of a treaty that would prevent the United States from possibly deploying weapons in outer space. On February 12, 2008, they jointly submitted a draft treaty that would prohibit the deployment of some weapons—including U.S. defensive missile interceptors—in outer space, while not affecting ground-based ICBMs that fly through space or conventional satellites that can be maneuvered to function as kinetic weapons against other satellites.[123]

Despite their overlapping interests in countering U.S. military activities in space, Russia has been very circumspect in cooperating with China's defense program. On December 26, 2006, the head of RosKosmos, Anatoly Perminov, acknowledged that the Russian Federation had an established policy of not sharing advanced space technologies with China for fear of creating a formidable future competitor. According to Perminov, though the Chinese space program may lag decades behind that of Russia and the United States, and still employs Soviet-era technologies, they were "quickly catching up." He said Russia would cooperate on joint projects, such as exploring the moon or supporting the International Space Station, but would not sell or otherwise transfer space-related technologies to China.[124]

The Russian position likely reflects recognition that many aerospace technologies have direct military applications. For example, China could use imported space technologies to develop improved military reconnaissance satellites or long-range ballistic missiles. In a future scenario, China might even use ASATs to threaten Russia's military assets in space. Alexander Khramchikhin, head of the analytical department at the Institute for Political and Military Analysis, interpreted the Chinese ASAT test in January 2007 as a threat to both Russia and the United States, since the Chinese were able to demonstrate a direct-ascent technology never tested by either Moscow or Washington.[125]

Russian authorities have not hesitated to punish Russian scientists (most notoriously physicist Valentin Danilov) who have violated export controls for proscribed technology. In November 2006, the Russian Federal Security Service (FSB) arrested several employees at the Tsniimash-Export Company, including the General Director Igor Reshetin, for selling to the China Precision Machinery Import-Expert Corporation—without Russian government approval—technology that could be used to create missile delivery systems. Tsniimash-Export is a leading Russian manufacturer of rockets and missiles that works closely with the Russian Space Agency. It also deals with customers in China and, until being sanctioned by the U.S. Government under the Iran Non-Proliferation Act in 2003, in the United States.[126]

Russian leaders also presumably do not want to jeopardize their country's extensive collaboration with the United States in civilian space activities, as well as potential opportunities for cooperating with NATO countries on certain aspects of space defense, by associating so closely with Beijing's defense program that Moscow's western partners might come to fear that any sensitive technologies they supplied Russia would soon find their way to China. Russian officials are undoubtedly aware that the Chinese ASAT test has generated efforts, especially within the U.S. Congress, to tighten international restrictions on the transfer of sensitive aerospace technologies to China.[127] After the Chinese ASAT test, the United States effectively suspended almost all the cooperative space programs agreed to between Presidents George Bush and Hu Jintao during their April 2006 summit meeting.[128] When Foreign Minister Lavrov returned from an early February 2007 visit to Washington, he stressed the Russian government's continued interest in cooperating with the United States in space exploration, including implementing some bilateral agreements that "could be linked with plans on military use of space."[129]

CENTRAL ASIA

Central Asia perhaps represents the geographic region where the security interests of China and Russia most overlap. Although the two countries often compete for Central Asian energy resources and commercial opportunities, their shared security interests mean that, for the most part, the newly independent states of Central Asia—Kazakhstan, Kyrgyzstan, Tajikistan, Turkmenistan, and Uzbekistan (the "Stans")—have not become venues for rivalry between Moscow and Beijing, as was once expected, but rather major unifying elements in Chinese-Russian relations. Nevertheless, this harmony arises primarily because Beijing views the region as of lower strategic priority than does Moscow, which still considers Central Asia a region of special Russian influence. China's growing interest in securing Central Asian oil and gas could lead Beijing to reconsider its policy of regional deference.

Russian Goals.

Even after the disintegration of the Soviet Union in 1991, Moscow has retained extensive political, economic, and security ties with the Stans. Russia's military assets in the region, especially its military bases in Kyrgyzstan and Tajikistan, also give it substantial hard power. During the last few years, the Russian government has been increasing its defense-related activities in Central Asia. In October 2003, it established its first new military base since the USSR's demise at Kant in Kyrgyzstan. As a result, Kyrgyzstan has become the only country hosting both a Russian and an American military base on its territory. The approximately 20 military aircraft and 500 troops deployed there lie only some 30 kilometers (20 miles) from the U.S. base at Manas, which is also used by some U.S. allies with military contingents in Afghanistan. The stated purpose of the Russian base is to protect Kyrgyzstan and other Collective Security Treaty Organization (CSTO) countries from external aggression, including foreign terrorist attacks.

Russian economic goals in Central Asia include ensuring that its firms participate in developing the region's energy resources and that Central Asian oil and gas exporters continue to use Russian pipelines. At present, Russian companies and business groups control much of the transportation systems for Central Asia's oil, gas, and electricity. Thanks to the legacy of the integrated Soviet economy, Central Asia's landlocked states continue to rely heavily on transportation, communications, supply-chain, and other networks that either traverse Russia or fall under Russian control. Although Russian firms have made some progress in developing suppliers in Russia to replace or supplement sources in other former Soviet states, many companies still rely on Central Asian suppliers for essential natural resources, equipment, and other inputs.

Central Asian manufacturers remain similarly dependent on Russian spare parts, technology, and services. The Russian government derives substantial tax and transit revenue from Russian business activities in Central Asia. Controlling the flow of Central Asian oil enhances Russia's leverage over foreign purchasers. In the case of natural gas, Central Asian supplies appear necessary to make up for shortfalls in existing export capacity. At present, Russia can purchase natural gas from Central Asia and resell it to European markets at over 100 percent markup.[130] The recent surge in world oil and gas prices has facilitated a major resurgence of Russian public and private investment in Central Asia.

Moscow also wants ethnic Russians in the region to be treated well, if only to prevent their mass immigration to Russia as burdensome refugees. Russia's higher standard of living already pulls millions of migrants from Central Asia into the Russian labor market, especially in the booming construction industry. Only a small percentage of these immigrants have obtained official permission to work in Russia, where even documented workers of Central Asian ethnicity encounter discrimination and abuse. Their remittances make an essential contribution to the gross national product (GNP) of their countries of origin, remove potentially dissatisfied social elements from these states, and give Central Asian governments another reason to stay on Moscow's good side.[131]

For at least the next few years, Russia will continue to derive soft power from its Soviet legacy. Although members of the younger generations in Central Asia are often drawn either to the West's consumer culture or toward Islamic movements, the region's predominantly secular and elderly political elite still sees Moscow as their lodestone. They appreciate Russian culture, have studied in Russia's prestigious schools, and follow court life in Moscow with rapt attention. Russian television, films, and newspapers still enjoy a substantial presence in Central Asia, while American products, including even Hollywood movies, remain surprisingly scarce.[132] The continued influence of the Russian language became evident in April 2001, when most of the heads of state attending the first summit of "Turkish-speaking" countries used Russian.[133] In several Central Asian countries, the Russian language is holding its own or even making a modest comeback.[134] The relocation of millions of Central Asian nationals to Russia during both the Soviet era and the post-independence period means that many families have friends and relatives in Russia. Thousands of military personnel from Central Asian armed forces study or train in Russia, often at subsidized rates. Local business elites are also typically more comfortable speaking Russian than English or Chinese.

Chinese Objectives.

China has had ties for centuries with Central Asia, but Russian and Soviet control of the region since the 19th century largely severed these contacts. Since the USSR's demise in 1991, China has reemerged as a major player in the region. In the realm of politics, Chinese authorities worry most about the spread of hostile ideologies such as liberal democracy and Islamic fundamentalism in Central Asia, both for their direct local effects and for their potential spillover consequences for Chinese territory. Fears of ethnic separatism in China's Xinjiang Uighur Autonomous Region reinforce this latter concern. It is a region, constituting one-sixth of China, where nationalists' uprisings marked by deadly violence occurred during the late 1980s and 1990s. Although massive immigration by Han Chinese into Xinjiang in recent decades has reduced the percentage of Muslim Uighurs in Xinjiang to below 50 percent of the 18 million people living there, the Uighurs enjoy ethnic and religious links to neighboring Turkic populations in Central Asia.[135] For example, approximately one million ethnic Kazakhs live in Xinjiang. Some of the members of the Uighur Diaspora in Central Asia, which numbers approximately half a million people, have been active in groups seeking an independent East Turkistan that would include Xinjiang.[136]

China has relied on diplomatic initiatives and security and other assistance to induce Central Asian governments to curb separatist activities by Uighur or "East Turkestan" activists, especially in Kazakhstan, Kyrgyzstan, and Uzbekistan. By 2004, Beijing had signed bilateral counterterrorism agreements with all four of its Central Asian neighbors with provisions including joint law enforcement operations, police training, and enhanced intelligence sharing.[137] The governments of Kazakhstan and Kyrgyzstan have both deported Uighurs following Chinese requests.[138] For its part, China has supplied Central Asian governments with some defense equipment, military training, and intelligence data to assist them to combat local "terrorist" groups.

China's growing energy needs represent another force driving its increased interest and involvement in Central Asia. A combination of a booming economy and declining domestic energy production has resulted in

China's importation of an increasingly large percentage of its oil and natural gas. Although China still acquires the bulk of its oil imports from the Persian Gulf and Africa, Chinese policymakers have sought to enhance their access to energy resources from Central Asia as well as Russia. Oil and gas from these regions can travel overland to China and obviate Beijing's reliance on vulnerable sea lanes susceptible to interception by the U.S. or other navies. In addition, the Chinese understand that terrorism, military conflicts, and other instability in the Middle East pose risks of disrupting its energy exports.

Although Central Asia currently provides only about 10 percent of China's total oil imports, Chinese planners apparently hope that by purchasing local energy equities and developing the region's eastward transportation infrastructure, they can increase this percentage substantially in the future.[139] In recent years, the Chinese government has been promoting the development of land-based oil and gas pipelines that would direct Central Asian energy resources eastwards towards China. Almost all of Central Asia's Soviet-era energy networks flow either westwards towards Europe or north to Russia.

Much of China's interest in developing Central Asia's energy resources has centered on Kazakhstan, its main trading partner in the region. In the first 6 months of 2007, the level of bilateral trade between China and Kazakhstan climbed to $5.97 billion, a figure more than 60 percent larger than that for the first half of 2006.[140] In July 2005, Chinese President Hu Jintao signed a declaration of strategic partnership with Kazakhstan President Nursultan Nazarbayev. Among other things, the agreement provided for expedited development of the 1,000-km Atasu-Alashankou pipeline that will transport at least 10 million tons of oil annually from Kazakhstan's Caspian coast to China's Xinjiang province, meeting as much as 15 percent of China's total demand for oil.[141] This 50-50 joint venture between the state-owned China National Petroleum Corporation (CNCP) and KazMunaiGaz, Kazakhstan's national oil and gas giant, began operating on a limited basis in December 2005, marking the first eastward flow of Central Asian oil and China's first import of oil by pipeline.[142] The CNCP has also acquired a substantial stake in a new natural gas field in western Kazakhstan.

When Hu Jintao visited Kazakhstan while returning to China after the August 16, 2007, SCO Bishkek summit, he and President Nazarbayev signed several energy agreements. One would expand an existing pipeline that carries oil from central Kazakhstan to China's Xinjiang province. The extension would transport oil from fields in Kazkahstan's Caspian Sea region to western China. The new line is scheduled to reach full capacity by 2011. The two presidents also announced that Kazkahstan would allow the natural gas pipeline being planned between Turkmenistan and China to pass through its territory. According to current plans, when completed in 2009, it will transport 30 billion cubic meters of gas to China annually. CNPC has already invested $6.5bn in oil projects in Kazakhstan and plans to increase that total, partially by developing fields in the Caspian region.[143]

Chinese planners have long envisioned constructing a 3,000-kilometer pipeline linking China to Kazakhstan's abundant Caspian Sea energy reserves. Following Kazakh President Nursultan Nazarbayev's visit to Beijing on December 20, 2006, the two sides launched a phased project to construct multiple oil pipelines—beginning first with an extension of the Atasu-Alashankou pipeline to the city of Kenkiyak in the Kazakh sector of the Caspian Sea—linking the two countries and financed by both.[144]

China also has begun developing energy ties with Uzbekistan and Turkmenistan. In July 2005, China's Sinopec negotiated a memorandum on cooperation with Uzbekneftegaz, Uzbekistan's state-owned energy company, that should entail China's investment of over $100 million during the next 5 years in the smaller country's oil industry.[145] In June 2006, China's National Oil and Gas Exploration Development Corporation (CNODC) announced it would spend $210 million to search for energy in Uzbekistan.[146] In April 2007, the Chinese and Uzbek governments released a statement announcing their intention to construct a 500-kilometer natural gas pipeline between their countries, with an annual capacity of 30 billion cubic meters (bcm) per year. This huge volume would amount to half of Uzbekistan's annual gas production. Since China and Uzbekistan do not border each other, the pipeline would need to traverse another Central Asian country.[147]

In April 2006, Chinese officials reached agreement with then President Saparmurat Niyazov of Turkmenistan to ship natural gas to China through a future pipeline. Current plans envisage the shipment next year of approximately 30 billion cubic meters of natural gas from Turkmenistan's Bagtyyarlyk field to Chinese markets through a 4,350-mile (7,000 kilometer) pipeline, continuing for at least 30 years.[148] For some time, Turkmenistan had been seeking alternative energy export routes to reduce its overwhelming dependence on Russian-owned pipelines.[149]

Besides securing access to the region's energy resources, Chinese officials also desire to enhance commerce between its relatively impoverished northwestern regions and their Central Asian neighbors. This consideration applies particularly to restless Xinjiang, whose Tarim Basin could supply over one-fifth of China's total oil consumption by 2010.[150] The Chinese government is developing new rail, pipeline, and other infrastructure links that would tighten the nexus between Xinjiang and both Central Asia and the rest of China.[151] Over half the province's foreign trade already derives from commerce with Central Asian countries.[152]

Trade across China's other borders with Central Asia also has been increasing, albeit starting from very low levels. The Chinese government has granted hundreds of millions of dollars in credits to the Central Asian countries for the purchase of Chinese goods. Its products—which are of higher quality than those from Russia and less expensive than Western imports—have established a major presence in the region's market for low-end consumer goods, machinery, and equipment.[153]

Despite the recent growth in commerce, neither China nor Central Asia ranks as a leading aggregate trading partner of the other. In 2006, the combined trade volume of Tajikistan, Uzbekistan, Kazakhstan, and Kyrgyzstan with China barely exceeded $10 billion.[154] Most of this commerce is centered on Kazakhstan. In 2006, China was the third largest purchaser of Kazakhstan's goods and the second largest seller after Russia.[155] Kyrgyzstan now also receives over half its imports from China, but accounts for only a small share of Chinese purchases.

Although formal Chinese companies have long replaced the private shuttle traders that pioneered transborder commerce, further increases in Chinese economic intercourse with or through Central Asia will require major improvements in the capacity and security of the region's east-west transportation links. A legacy of the formerly integrated Soviet economy is that most roads, railways, and energy pipelines flow northward towards Russia. Beijing is currently funding several major infrastructure projects to spur east-west traffic, including energy pipelines, communications and power networks, and improved roads and railroads.[156] For example, the Chinese are hoping that construction will begin in 2008 on two new railways connecting Xinjiang with Kazakhstan, Kyrgyzstan, and Uzbekistan.[157] China has made available a $900 million loan to SCO member states on easy terms to finance projects for developing Central Asia's natural resources and infrastructure.

In the realm of soft power, Chinese leaders face certain impediments in Central Asia. Knowledge of the Chinese language is far less common in Central Asia than that of Russian or even English. Many Central Asians, especially those in border communities near Xingjiang, fear being swamped by China's enormous population through immigration.[158] For comparison, Kazakhstan's entire population amounts to approximately 1 percent of that of China. Central Asians also commonly complain about the poor quality of imported Chinese consumer goods. On the other hand, many Central Asian leaders admire their Chinese counterparts' ability to achieve high rates of economic growth while preserving their authoritarian political system.

Shared Chinese-Russian Interests.

Although China and Russia often compete for Central Asian energy supplies and commercial opportunities, the two governments share a desire to limit instability in the region. They especially fear ethnic separatism in their border territories supported by Islamic fundamentalist movements in Central Asia. Russian authorities dread the prospect of continued instability in the northern Caucasus, particularly Chechnya and neighboring Dagestan. China's leaders worry about separatist agitation in Xinjiang.

The current governments of both Russia and China are clearly uneasy over the substantial U.S. military presence in Central Asia as well as American democracy promotion activities in the region. When the onset of Operation ENDURING FREEDOM in late 2001 brought large numbers of American combat troops to Russia's southern border, the divided Russian political and military elite found solace in the compromise formulation that the U.S. forces should stay only for the duration of the antiterrorist campaign, implying a long but not indefinite period. This reluctant acceptance of the U.S. military presence reflected a grudging recognition that the Americans could destroy Russia's Islamic extremist enemies and promote regional stability more effectively than Russia could by itself due to its reduced capabilities.[159]

More recently, the regional instability following from the U.S. invasion of Iraq and the "color revolutions" that have seen the deposition of pro-Moscow governments around Russia's borders have led many influential Russians to see the U.S. presence as a major source of instability in its own right.[160] In August 2005, Deputy Foreign Minister Grigorii Karasin warned that the "enforcement of democracy" in the former Soviet Union would engender instability and unpredictable consequences throughout the region.[161] In June 2006, President Putin expressed understanding for Uzbekistan's decision the previous year to expel U.S. military forces from its territory, observing that Washington had only itself to blame by behaving like a "bull in a china shop" in the region, i.e., by publicly decrying the host country's authoritarian excesses.[162]

Chinese leaders have also expressed concern over external democracy promotion efforts in Eurasia. In July 2006, Chinese President Hu Jinato echoed Putin in warning against foreign interference in countries' internal affairs: "We hope the outside world will accept the social system and path to development independently chosen by our members ... and respect the domestic and foreign policies adopted by the SCO participants in line with their national conditions."[163] Chinese analysts have described Western governments as supporting anti-Chinese terrorist movements in Central Asia under the fig leaf of democracy promotion.[164]

Russian and Chinese leaders have avoided directly challenging the American military presence in Central Asia. Their ambivalence reflects recognition of the advantages of having the United States suppress the region's terrorist movements and promote the stability required to develop Central Asian oil and gas resources. It also results from uncertainties over the ability of China and Russia to manage the consequences of a complete and rapid U.S. military disengagement from the region. Recall that the precipitous Soviet withdrawal from Afghanistan as their empire crumbled created a major security vacuum in the region that disrupted economic and political stability in neighboring countries for at least a decade.

Chinese-Russian Conflicts.

Despite the overlapping interests of Russia and China in Central Asia, their policies in that region still frequently conflict. Russian officials have actively opposed Chinese efforts to acquire majority ownership of Central Asian energy assets, preferring that these resources remain under the control of Russia's powerful energy companies or Central Asia's pliant national governments. The Russian government has also worked to prevent the establishment of a SCO-wide free trade zone, which would allow cheap Chinese goods to swamp local markets.

One reason why the Russian government has made only modest efforts to constrain Washington's influence in Central Asia is that the U.S. engagement in the region helps reassure Russians anxious about how China's growing economic and military power will affect regional politics. In 2006, Deputy Secretary of the Russian Security Council Nikolai Spassky said that East Asia's transformation "could pose the most important challenge to Russia's national security for the next decades." He emphasized, however, that this challenge would become a threat only if Russia ignored or failed to adequately respond to developments there.[165] Russia's membership in the SCO presumably helps ensure that Moscow remains involved in Eurasian security issues, but the American presence serves as an added safeguard.

Russian strategists have sought to preserve at least one major asymmetry regarding China's presence in Central Asia. Unlike Russia and the United States, China lacks permanent bases in Central Asia outside Chinese territory and has not offered defense security guarantees to any Central Asian government. The Chinese armed forces do engage in frequent bilateral and multilateral military and internal security exercises in the region, but the Chinese participants have always returned home upon their conclusion. As its overall military modernization proceeds, however, China's ability to project power into nearby Central Asia correspondingly increases.[166]

There is some evidence that the Russian government has taken steps to counter or control any potential Chinese military presence in the region. When the pro-Beijing government of President Askar Akayev came under threat in neighboring Kyrgyzstan in late May 2005, Foreign Ministry spokesperson Liu Jianchao said China would "seriously consider" deploying troops, perhaps under the auspices of the SCO, to southern Kyrgyzstan to help counter "terrorism, separatism, and extremism" there.[167] However, according to some sources, Russian and local opposition blocked the deployment.[168] In late July 2005, the acting Deputy Prime Minister of the new Kyrgyz government said: "The deployment of a Chinese military base on Kyrgyz territory has been discussed at a very high level, but Bishkek will not turn the national territory into a military and political range. We have enough means and forces to protect the sovereignty of Kyrgyzstan."[169] Kyrgyz officials alleviated Chinese concerns by reaffirming their commitments to the SCO and to oppose terrorism, separatism, and extremism.

Russian-Chinese commercial competition in Central Asia is even more evident. In September 2004, Chinese Prime Minster Wen Jiabao proposed establishing a comprehensive common market within the SCO that would affect members' trade, customs, tax, immigration, and other policies. Russian officials, fearful that an inflow of cheap Chinese goods and services would drive Russian enterprises out of the region, argued that economic integration among SCO nations should occur gradually, over the course of decades—thus conveniently preserving Russian economic domination over Central Asia in the interim.[170]

Russia and China also have cross-cutting interests with respect to oil and gas. Both countries want to increase Central Asian production. Russia, however, wants to maintain control over these sources as well as the region's energy transportation infrastructure in order to divert deliveries to privileged buyers or, if world prices are low, to stockpile supplies. As a major energy consumer, however, China desires to exert direct control over regional energy assets—preferably by purchasing them outright—and maximize production regardless of the effects on world energy prices. The two countries are now engaged in direct competition for Turkmenistan's large but problematic gas supplies.[171]

THE SHANGHAI COOPERATION ORGANIZATION

China's and Russia's overlapping and diverging interests in Central Asia have manifested themselves most visibly in the SCO. Since its founding in 2001, the SCO has essentially functioned as a Chinese-Russian condominium, providing Beijing and Moscow with a convenient multilateral framework to manage their interests in the newly independent countries of Central Asia. At present, Kazakhstan, Kyrgyzstan, Tajikistan, and Uzbekistan are also full members, while India, Iran, Mongolia, and Pakistan have observer status in the organization.

History.

The SCO emerged from a series of border security negotiations begun in November 1992 between Beijing and the former Soviet republics located along China's border (Kazakhstan, Kyrgyzstan, and Tajikistan, as well as Russia). Starting in 1996, the five countries began to hold annual summit meetings as the "Shanghai Five." At the first leadership summit meeting in Shanghai on April 26, 1996, the governments signed a "Treaty on Deepening Military Trust in Border Regions," which established a set of military confidence-building measures along their shared borders. During the second meeting of the five nations under this framework, which occurred in Moscow on April 25, 1997, they signed a "Treaty on Reduction of Military Forces in Border Regions" that restricted conventional military deployments and activities within a hundred kilometer-wide demilitarized zone along these common borders.

Subsequent Shanghai Five summits began to discuss economic and other nonmilitary issues, including how to cope with regional terrorism, narcotics trafficking, and other transnational threats of concern to all the participating states. By 2001, the governments involved decided they needed a more permanent mechanism to address their expanding multilateral agenda. In particular, they sought more frequent meetings than the annual leadership summits and expansion of the range of government agencies to encompass security, law enforcement, economic, and others. At their June 2001 meeting, the Shanghai Five joined with Uzbekistan, whose president had attended the July 2000 summit in Dushanbe as an observer, to institutionalize their interactions by establishing the SCO, replacing the Shanghai Five.[172]

Building on the arms control achievements of the Shanghai Five as discussed above, the SCO has sponsored extensive, senior-level consultations on several issues, including crime, narcotics trafficking, economic development, transportation, communication, energy, the war in Afghanistan, and terrorism. The latter topic has become the most important issue of concern for its members. The parties are establishing concrete mechanisms to facilitate such cooperation—including annual meetings of their defense, foreign, and prime ministers—as well as formal structures to interact with nonmember governments and other international institutions.

Security Role.

Since 2003, the SCO has sponsored a number of "antiterrorist exercises" involving paramilitary as well as intelligence and law enforcement personnel. In October 2002, China and Kyrgyzstan conducted the first bilateral antiterror exercise within the SCO framework, involving joint border operations by hundreds of troops. It marked the PLA's first maneuvers with another country's military. In August 2003, all the member government militaries, with the exception of those from Uzbekistan, participated in the first formal SCO-sponsored combined exercise (*Cooperation 2003*). It involved over 1,000 troops engaging in several counterterrorism scenarios in eastern Kazakhstan and China's Xinjiang region.[173] During the unprecedented Russian-Chinese military exercises of August 2005, all six SCO defense or deputy defense ministers attended as observers. American and other Western representatives were not invited. Later Assistant Secretary of Defense for International Security Affairs Peter Rodman said that Washington had wanted to observe the exercise, but "the Chinese declined to invite us."[174] In early March 2006, Uzbekistan affirmed its heightened commitment to the SCO by hosting a multilateral exercise under its auspices, *East-Antiterror-2006*. Representatives from the member governments' special services and law enforcement personnel rehearsed hostage rescue and defense of critical infrastructure from terrorist attacks.[175]

The language used inthe fifth anniversary declaration of the SCO, adapted in June 2006, resembles that found in standard nonaggression pacts. Members pledge not to join alliances or otherwise take actions that would "allow their territories to be used to undermine the sovereignty, security, or territorial integrity of the other member states." It also provides for immediate consultations during "emergencies that threaten regional peace, stability, and security." Lastly, the declaration indicates interest in signing a SCO multilateral "treaty of good-neighborliness" and creating a regional conflict prevention mechanism.[176]

The SCO gained notoriety in the West in July 2005, when the governments of Russia, China, and most Central Asian countries unexpectedly called on the United States and its allies to set a timetable for ending their military presence in the region.[177] That act prompted General Richard Myers, then Chairman of the U.S. Joint Chiefs of Staff, to accuse Moscow and Beijing of "trying to bully" their smaller neighbors into weakening security ties with Washington.[178] Many observers suspect that Russian and Chinese representatives at the July 2005 SCO summit encouraged Uzbekistan to expel U.S. military forces from its territory and subsequently pressured Kyrgyzstan to end U.S. access to the air force base at Manas airport as well.[179] A steady stream of senior U.S. officials visited the Kyrgyz capital before the August 2007 SCO summit to dissuade officials from making U.S. access to the Manas base an issue at the gathering.[180]

A series of bizarre incidents—the December 2006 killing of a Kyrgyz worker by a U.S. airman, a mysterious kidnapping of an American female soldier, and a ground collision between a taxiing U.S. airplane and the Kyrgyz presidential jet—have soured much of the population on the 1,000-man American presence.[181] Members of the Kyrgyz parliament—prompted by local mass news media outlets and various pro-Russian nongovernment organization (NGO) activists—pressed the government to evict U.S. forces from the base.[182] For the time being, however, the Kyrgyz government has said it will support the United States as long as the war in Afghanistan continues (and after the United States agreed in July 2006 to increase its yearly compensation payments from $20 million to $150 million).[183] In addition, the recent resurgence of the Taliban in Afghanistan has apparently dampened Chinese-Russian interest in precipitating a rapid Western military withdrawal.

Instead, the SCO has become more engaged in developing the capacity to protect its nondemocratic member governments against internal as well as external challenges.[184] Unlike the Organization for Security and Cooperation in Europe (OSCE), the EU, and NATO, the SCO has long explicitly adhered to the principle of "noninterference" in domestic affairs, which in practice has meant not requiring members to respect international civil rights standards. After perceived election improprieties served as the immediate trigger for the color revolutions in Georgia and Ukraine (resulting in deposition of entrenched old-guard governments), the SCO formed its own cadre of election observers. Since their first use during the February 2005 ballot in Kyrgyzstan, they have endorsed every election held in a member state, with the notable exception of the victory of the pro-Western candidate, Victor Yushchenko, in Ukraine's 2004 presidential elections.[185] Along with the traditionally compliant monitors organized by the Commonwealth of Independent States (CIS), the SCO observers help bolster the legitimacy of Central Asia's authoritarian regimes by having another prominent international institution certify even questionable results.

The latest exercise, *Peace Mission 2007*, occurred during the period August 8-17, 2007. This was the largest SCO joint exercise in the organization's 6-year history. Almost 6,500 troops and 80 aircraft participated in the two phases, including 2,000 troops from Russia and 1,600 from China.[186] As in 2005, the organizers declined to allow American observers at the event.[187] The first phase of the exercise occurred in Russia's Volga-Urals Military District, the second phase at Urumqi, capital of Xinjiang. The latter location led some observers to charge that "the real objective" of the exercise was "to intimidate the Uighur population in East Turkestan and to warn the democratic forces in Central Asia not to challenge the authoritarian regimes."[188] In addition, the scenario for *Peace Mission 2007*—as well as the thousands of troops with accompanying warplanes and other heavy military equipment—seems designed to enhance the ability of the participating armed forces to suppress another attempt at a popular rebellion such as the one that occurred in Andijon, Uzbekistan, in 2005. At the time, the SCO was not capable of organizing a military intervention to repress the uprising, which appears to have involved both citizens dissatisfied with the government's policies as well as anti-regime militants. Since then, the SCO has tried to develop such a capacity.

Afghanistan.

Afghanistan is emerging as a potential area of future joint engagement by Russia and China, primarily under the auspices of the SCO. At its August 2007 summit in Bishkek, several SCO governments identified narcotics trafficking from Afghanistan as a major regional security problem. In their Bishkek Declaration on international security, the summit participants expressed alarm over "the threat of narcotics coming from Afghanistan and its negative effect on Central Asia" and called for "combining international efforts on the creation of antinarcotics belts around Afghanistan." The heads of state also affirmed their readiness "to participate in the efforts to normalize the political situation in Afghanistan" and "to develop economic cooperation with the country." In addition, the communiqué issued by the heads of state called for greater use of "the SCO—Afghanistan Contact Group mechanism as well as other mutually acceptable formats" to manage Afghan-related security threats.

Shortly before the summit, the Russian Foreign Ministry circulated a draft proposal for an international conference on Afghanistan that, while under SCO auspices, would nevertheless include interested countries from both the region and elsewhere. In his speech to the summit attendees, Russian President Vladimir Putin urged the foreign ministries of the SCO members to take charge of organizing such a gathering. He also called on the SCO to create a counternarcotics security zone around Afghanistan that would help monitor money laundering and other sources of terrorist financing associated with Afghan narcotics trafficking.

Although China is not situated along the "Northern Route" through which Afghan narcotics have traditionally entered Central Asia and Europe, new narcotics trafficking networks have developed since 2005 that transport illicit drugs from Afghanistan through Pakistan and Central Asia into China. In addition, Chinese officials remain concerned about the Taliban's ties with Islamic extremist groups advocating independence for China's Xinjiang Uighur Autonomous Region. A June 2007 *People's Daily* commentary warned that,

> The "Taliban phenomenon" has produced grave concern . . . its resurgence has severely challenged the authority of the Afghan government . . . the Taliban have grown more robust . . . taking full advantage of local feelings of dissatisfaction over living conditions and anti-U.S. sentiments . . . the Taliban have galvanized their link-up with al-Qaeda remnants . . . Afghanistan is at risk of becoming the second Iraq.

An official at the Chinese Foreign Ministry subsequently said that, since maintaining stability in the larger Central Asian region represented a "primary focus" of the SCO, China and other member governments want to cooperate in fighting drug smuggling and terrorism emanating from Afghanistan.

Energy Aspirations.

Several SCO governments have proposed establishing some kind of energy bloc within the institution. The organization's current roster of full member nations and observers does include some of the world's leading energy suppliers (Russia and Iran) and consumers (China and India). The present lack of strong international energy institutions linking the major energy supplier and consumer countries in Eurasia could provide an opening for the SCO to assume this role.

Any such club would differ from the Organization of Petroleum Exporting Countries (OPEC) in three essential respects. First, it would include energy importers as well as exporters. Second, its membership would be regional rather than global. Third, as a result of these limitations, it would probably serve predominately as a mechanism for dialogue rather than setting quotas or fixing prices.

Also to be emphasized, the cross-cutting interests among these countries seem likely to impede the SCO's ability to achieve its full potential in the energy realm. The SCO's two most influential members have fundamentally different interests in this sector. Although both Russia and China desire to increase Central Asian oil and gas production, Moscow wants to maintain its control over these assets as well as the region's energy transportation infrastructure. The response of Russian government representatives to China's recent energy deals in Central Asia made clear their concerns. In August 2007, Andrei Denisov, Russia's First Deputy Minister of Foreign Affairs, acknowledged that Russia could not exclude China from Central Asian energy markets, just as Beijing could not displace Russia entirely, since "the presence of the two countries there is organic." Instead, he maintained that "the main thing in this respect is, considering the factor of competition, to cut down the aggregate expenditure on the development of energy resources, and ensure a fair distribution of them for delivery to the world markets." For this reason, Denisov argued that China's recent long-term energy supply agreements with Kazakhstan and Turkmenistan "must be integrated into a mutually beneficial and mutually acceptable pattern."[189]

In conflict with Russia's insistence on maintaining control, China, a major energy consumer, desires to exert direct supervision over regional energy assets. While the Russian government is pushing for a unified multilateral SCO energy bloc, which Moscow could dominate through its powerful state-run energy companies, Beijing persists in pursuing bilateral deals that would redirect Central Asian oil and gas eastward rather than into Russia.

Russian-Chinese differences are also evident in their approach to SCO's developing security role. Whereas the Chinese appear preoccupied with averting future Tiananmen-like rebellions, the Russian high command envisages a possible need to fight another Chechnya-style counterinsurgency operation. In addition, Russian officials apparently hope to strengthen the SCO's role as a military institution in order to extend its influence over the national militaries of its other members, including China. Yet, Russia's aspirations in this regard have not been realized until now because of the opposition of China and apparently some Central Asian states to transforming the SCO into a quasi-military alliance. These governments prefer an organization whose main purpose is antiterrorism (i.e., internal rather than external security) and economic cooperation rather than politicized anti-Americanism. Chinese representatives have shown little interest in Russian proposals to deepen military ties between the SCO and the Moscow-dominated CSTO, which includes all other SCO countries except China.

Expansion Problems.

Another difference between Russia and China concerns the issue of expanding SCO membership further. The SCO currently has a complex organizational structure with participating countries arranged according to the three general categories of full members, formal observers, and "guests of honor" selected by the rotating hosting government of the annual SCO leadership summit. The current roster of full members includes only those six states that joined the organization at its founding in 2001. In June 2004, Mongolia became the first formal SCO observer. At the organization's July 2005 summit in Shanghai, India, Iran, and Pakistan achieved formal observer status as well. Though the specific rights and duties of SCO observers have never been clear, their status appeared to grant them the right to attend major SCO meetings (such as the annual heads of state summit), but not the right to vote when decisions were made. In addition, representatives of the full SCO members often hold meetings among themselves that exclude observer participation. At the Bishkek summit, for example, the heads of the six full SCO members met alone before inviting SCO observers as well as the honored guests to join them.[190]

The precise number of countries seeking to obtain full membership or observer status in the SCO is unclear. Some governments, such as Azerbaijan, have expressed an interest in principle in cooperating with the SCO, but have yet to take any concrete steps in this direction.[191] Others, such as Nepal, are already seeking a more formal institutional relationship. The country's acting Foreign Secretary, Gyan Chandra Acharya, has stated that Nepal wants to join as an observer.[192]

Immediately before the June 2006 Shanghai summit, Chinese Assistant Foreign Minister Li Hui stated that "a lot of countries in Asia and other continents have applied, demonstrating the SCO is broadening its influence."[193] At that summit, however, the SCO declined to expand the number of formal members. The putative reason was that the members had not yet worked out the legal basis for such expansion.[194] In 2007, Kyrgyz Foreign Ministry official Astanbek Osmonaliyev likewise said that a number of governments were requesting observer status.[195] At the summit, all the existing members decided to keep the moratorium in effect "for some time yet."[196]

The most plausible new SCO full members are those countries already enjoying close ties with the SCO. The Mongolian member has not indicated any strong interest recently in becoming a full SCO member.[197] Most present members appear to consider Mongolia too distant from Central Asia to warrant full membership in any case. At the Bishkek summit, Mongolian President Nambaryn Enkhbayar spoke only of intensifying cooperation with the SCO within the framework of his country's current nonmember status: "We hope that after the revision of the document on the status of observer countries and the adoption of a plan of cooperation with them . . . new possibilities will be created for involving observer countries in the SCO's activities."[198]

Of the remaining countries, Iran and Pakistan seem most eager to become full SCO members. Iran's most important institutional ties in Central Asia are those with the SCO. Iran is not a member of any Euro-Atlantic security institution that arose to manage the Cold War or its aftermath, so Tehran vigorously sought observer status in the SCO, which it gained in July 2005. Iranian and SCO objectives overlap in several areas, especially energy. Yet, any proposal to grant Iran full SCO membership would prove highly controversial, given Iran's policies regarding Israel, nuclear proliferation, and regional terrorism.

Thanks to strong Chinese backing, Pakistan finally received formal observer status in the SCO at its July 2005 summit, after having applied for full membership in September 2000. During a mid-March 2007 trip to Uzbekistan, Pakistani Prime Minister Shaukat Aziz reaffirmed Pakistan's desire to become a "full-fledged" member. In the past, however, other governments have expressed reservations about increasing security ties with Pakistan, given its links with the Taliban insurgency in neighboring Afghanistan. Although Islamabad's relations with Russia, India, and the Central Asian states have warmed in recent years, only China appears to strongly support granting it full SCO membership.

At present, neither Beijing nor Moscow appears eager to grant Tehran full membership either, given the explosive reaction this would provoke in Western countries. They also both seem interested in incorporating gas-rich Turkmenistan into the SCO now that its new government seems more open to participation in Eurasian multinational institutions. However, Beijing and Moscow continue to differ on whether Pakistan—China's close ally but seen by many other SCO nations as too closely linked to the region's terrorist movements—or India—Russia's favorite but still seen in Beijing as an unwelcome rival in Central Asia—should join.

KOREA

China and Russia share a concern with the evolving political, military, and economic situation on the Korean peninsula, which borders both countries. In all these dimensions, however, the two governments have thus far pursued largely independent but parallel policies toward both North and South Korea, with Beijing assuming a clear lead role and Moscow often struggling to maintain even a supporting position.

Shared Anxieties Regarding Korea.

China and Russia share a concern with the evolving political, military, and economic situation on the nearby Korean peninsula. During the Korean War, the two countries jointly backed the Democratic People's Republic of Korea (DPRK) regime with armaments, military advisers, and, in the case of China, hundreds of thousands of armed "volunteers." After the Sino-Soviet alliance collapsed in the late 1950s, the two countries competed for influence in Pyongyang. Beijing usually emerged preeminent, but both governments were frustrated with the unpredictable and reflexively xenophobic North Korean leadership. The DPRK regime finely balanced relations with its two great power patrons to receive aid from both without committing to either. Today, although China and Russia share many objectives regarding the Korean peninsula, they continue to pursue largely independent policies.

China and Russia have both opposed North Korea's acquisition of nuclear weapons while simultaneously resisting international antinuclear initiatives that they believe could create chaos on the peninsula. Both Beijing and Moscow desire a change in Pyongyang's behavior but not a change in its regime. They remain more concerned over the potential collapse of the North Korean state than over its government's intransigence on the nuclear question. Despite their differences with Kim Jong-il, Chinese and Russian leaders fear that North Korea's disintegration could induce widespread economic disruptions in East Asia, generate large refugee flows across their borders, weaken Chinese and Russian influence in the Koreas by ending their status as the main interlocutors with Pyongyang, and potentially remove a buffer separating their borders from American ground forces (i.e., should the U.S. Army ever redeploy into northern Korea). At worst, the DPRK's collapse could precipitate a military conflict on the peninsula—which could spill across into Chinese territory. Policymakers in both countries appear to have resigned themselves to dealing with Kim for now, while hoping a more accommodating leadership emerges eventually in Pyongyang.

From the perspective of Beijing and Moscow, an ancillary benefit of their present approach to North Korea is that it nicely coincides with that of the current South Korean government in many respects. Beijing, Moscow, and Seoul all oppose North Korea's acquisition of nuclear weapons, but also hope to coax the regime out of its self-destructive isolation without undue coercion. All three governments fear the chaos that might ensue from a rapid collapse of the regime in Pyongyang and, more or less openly, fear that any rash American actions might precipitate a war in their neighborhood. In hopes of avoiding such an outcome, they all advocate pursuing strategies that reassure North Korean leaders about their security. They also want to promote economic reform in North Korea while integrating the country into the broader East Asian economic community. Through these means, they hope to stabilize North Korea in the short term while moderating its foreign policies over the long term.

Although the UNSC passed a resolution condemning North Korea's October 9, 2006, nuclear test, opposition from Russia and especially China forced the United States and Japan to abandon their efforts to push through a more strongly worded resolution that might have authorized the use of force. Since Beijing and Moscow desire a change in Pyongyang's behavior but not a change in its regime, their delegations successfully insisted that UNSC Resolution 1718, adopted on October 14, aim less to punish North Korea retroactively than to modify its future policies. The resolution bans the transfer of material to North Korea related to its nuclear, ballistic missile, and unconventional weapons programs. It also freezes the foreign assets and prohibits international travel of those individuals involved in the DPRK's nuclear, ballistic missile, and other WMD programs along with their family members. Additional provisions prohibit the sale of all luxury goods to North Korea, and give all countries the right to inspect cargo moving to and from North Korea in order to enforce the resolution. UNSCR 1718 does not, however, authorize UN members to enforce its provisions with military action.[199]

Chinese and Russian leaders were clearly angered by Kim Jong-Il's defiance of Beijing's warnings against testing a nuclear weapon. Chinese sources claim that Pyongyang notified Beijing about the detonation only 20 minutes beforehand.[200] In response, the Chinese ostentatiously conducted some inspections of cross-border shipments and dispatched an envoy to Pyongyang to bring Kim Jong-Il back into the fold. Russian diplomats were even more vocal in their concerns. Warning Pyongyang not to conduct another test, Deputy Foreign Minister Alexander Losyukov said the DPRK's nuclear weapons program "threatened" Russia's interests.[201] On February 5, 2007, Russian Ambassador to South Korea Gleb Ivashentsov complained that "the site of the nuclear test by the DPRK on October 9, 2006, is situated at the distance of just 177 Kms [from] our border. We do not like that. We . . . need in the proximity of our borders neither nuclear and missile tests nor saber-rattling by anyone."[202] To ensure the country's nuclear disarmament, the Russian delegation to the Six-Party talks has demanded that the DPRK dismantle its nuclear facilities at Yongbyon rather than simply suspend operations there.[203]

Nevertheless, the Chinese and Russian governments remain more concerned about the potential immediate collapse of the North Korean state than about its leader's intransigence on the nuclear question. Despite their differences with the Kim regime, Chinese and Russian leaders recognize that the DPRK's disintegration could induce catastrophic consequences, to include precipitating a military conflict on the peninsula which could spill over across their borders.[204]

In principle, Russia could accommodate to North Korea's collapse more easily than China. Since Moscow has less robust bilateral relations with the two Koreas than many other countries do, any security interactions with both Koreas that do exist occur primarily within the frameworks provided by regional and international institutions such as the Six-Party Talks. Except for designation as chair of the regional security architecture working group established to implement the February 2007 Six-Party agreement—a working group whose ultimate impact and duration remain uncertain—Moscow does not have a leadership role in any of these bodies despite decades of Soviet and Russian proposals to create various multinational institutions in East Asia.

During most of the 1990s, Russian policymakers under President Boris Yeltsin shunned the DPRK while pursuing better ties with South Korea. Moscow played little role during the first Korean nuclear crisis in 1993-94. Despite its pioneering involvement in North Korea's nuclear energy program, Russia did not join the new Korean Peninsula Energy Development Organization (KEDO) consortium, a multinational group established to construct two light-water reactors as part of the 1994 Agreed Framework. Russia declined to renew the 1961 Soviet-North Korean Friendship and Mutual Assistance Treaty, which had a military intervention clause, when it expired in September 1996. With Russia lacking close ties with either Korea, its status regarding the peninsula's security affairs deteriorated during the 1990s to that of an interested observer, as was the case at the Four-Party Talks among China, the United States, and the two Koreas that began in September 1997.

Yeltsin's successor, Vladimir Putin, has tried to reestablish Russia's influence in East Asia, including North Korea. In February 2000, the two countries signed a new bilateral cooperation treaty, which provided for consultations in the case of mutual threats. Putin suffered an embarrassment, though, on the one occasion when he launched its own diplomatic initiative regarding the Korean crisis. In July 2000, a few days after visiting the DPRK, Putin announced at the G-8 Kyushu-Okinawa summit that Kim Jung-il had told him the DPRK was prepared to abandon its ballistic missile programs in return for international assistance in creating a civilian space program. The North Korean government disavowed Putin's declaration shortly thereafter.[205] Since then, Russian diplomats have sought a role in the regional peace process. The DPRK, seeking to reduce its dependence on Beijing, insisted on Moscow's presence in the Six-Party talks—but have not made the issue a major priority.[206]

Russia's overall economic stake in North Korea is minimal. Soviet leader Michael Gorbachev's decision to put all Soviet trade with socialist countries on a hard-currency footing, a practice continued by the Yeltsin administration, precipitated a sharp deterioration in commercial exchanges between the two countries. The level of bilateral trade, which predominately involves Russia's eastern regions, barely exceeded $200 million in 2006.[207] In recent years, Pyongyang's main export to Russia has been the thousands of expatriate North Korean workers in Russia's timber industry.

North Korean negotiators have indicated they wanted Moscow to write off the entire $8 billion debt the DPRK incurred during the Soviet period, and most Russians seem resigned to not seeing a ruble of repayment.[208] Russian negotiators agreed to waive most of it as an incentive to secure Pyongyang's return to Six-Party talks and to eliminate an obstacle to future economic cooperation.[209] Thus far, however, the unending Korean crisis has blocked the most potentially lucrative projects—plans to construct a trans-Korean railroad and connect it with the Trans-Siberian line, or to build energy pipelines between Russia and South Korea across North Korean territory.[210] Under Putin, Russia suspended all military sales to Pyongyang.[211]

Despite its modest ties with North Korea, Moscow would not welcome the abrupt collapse of the DPRK regime. Korean refugees could flow into the Russian Far East, worsening the region's already severe economic problems.[212] Most seriously, the DPRK's demise would likely reduce the substantial South Korean investment flows into Russia by redirecting them toward North Korea's rehabilitation and the peninsula's possible reunification (hoped-for Chinese investment capital would be less likely to materialize in this case as well). A military conflict on the peninsula, besides generating all the negative repercussions glanced at above, would involve fighting among nuclear powers near Russia's border, with the inevitable risk of unintended Russian casualties. Almost any conceivable war would worsen Russia's relations with some of the parties to the conflict. For this reason, Russians most favor applying the "Ukrainian model" to the nuclear crisis. In this scenario, Pyongyang would voluntarily surrender its nuclear weapons in return for economic assistance and security assurances from the other great powers.[213] After the October 2006 DPRK nuclear test, Putin declared it was important not to back North Korea into a corner and leave it with no option but to raise tensions—the same argument he later made regarding Iran.[214] Although Moscow's commercial and strategic ties are stronger with Tehran than with Pyongyang, the collapse of the DPRK regime would present more immediate problems for Russia given its proximity and its pivotal position on the security agenda of China, South Korea, and Japan.

While China also gains little from its economic intercourse with the DPRK, the latter's disintegration would present Beijing with an even more serious challenge in the near term, given China's greater dependence on flows of investment capital to East Asia and the presence of a larger Korean minority in China than in Russia. These considerations may partly explain why Chinese officials have adopted a higher profile than their Russian counterparts in managing the North Korean problem in recent years, especially through the Six-Party talks.[215] Beijing policymakers appear to have resigned themselves to dealing with Kim for now, while hoping a more accommodating DPRK leadership emerges eventually.

Chinese pressure, added to a change in U.S. policy that allowed for direct bilateral negotiations with DPRK representatives and with other concessions, helped secure an agreement at the end of the fifth round of the Six-Party Talks, which ended on February 13, 2007.[216] Under its terms, North Korea pledged to shut down and eventually dismantle its Yongbyon nuclear complex in return for food, economic aid, and the prospect of normalizing relations with the five other countries. The five working groups established to implement the February agreement have begun assessing how to achieve progress on the most important issues—U.S.-DPRK relations; Japan-DPRK relations; economic and energy cooperation; the regional security architecture; and North Korea's denuclearization. Chinese officials worked with their American counterparts to arrange for DPRK leaders to recover some of the millions in frozen funds held by the Bank of Macao.[217]

The long-term prospects of the February 13 agreement remain uncertain. The parties decided to postpone resolving some intractable issues, such as whether to provide the DPRK with civilian light-water reactors and what North Korea must do with its stockpile of atomic bombs, whose very number is uncertain.[218] These compromises resulted in an ambiguous, complex, multiphase deal that could unravel at many points and in many ways. Critics doubting whether the DPRK government will fulfill its commitments, complain that a better deal was achievable years earlier, before North Korea resumed plutonium reprocessing and tested an atomic bomb.[219] Nevertheless, the accord appears to have ended the immediate crisis and established the basis for expanding cooperation among the signatories in other areas. In defending the agreement, Secretary of State Condoleezza Rice stressed that, by working with China and through the mechanism of the Six-Party Talks, "We're building a set of relationships."[220]

Improving Republic of Korea Ties with China and Russia.

Chinese policymakers share many interests and objectives with their South Korean colleagues regarding the DPRK. Beijing and Seoul oppose North Korea's acquisition of nuclear weapons but also hope to coax the regime out of its self-destructive isolation. The DPRK's precipitous end would be an economic nightmare for both countries. It would drive investment capital away from the region while simultaneously requiring the two to undertake a costly humanitarian relief and economic reconstruction program. In addition, China and South Korea share a concern that North Korean policies are contributing to Japan's remilitarization.

Most importantly, South Korean leaders agree with their Chinese counterparts about the chaos that would ensue from a rapid collapse of the DPRK regime. The two countries would have to assume the main burden of providing immediate humanitarian relief and sustained economic assistance at a time when both would suffer the most from the deteriorating investment climate. Informed observers in both countries fear that rash American actions might precipitate a war in their backyard. In hopes of avoiding such an outcome, they mutually favor an approach that reassures the DPRK leadership about its security. They also want to promote economic reform in North Korea while integrating the country into the regional economy. Such developments could help stabilize North Korea in the short term while providing incentives and leverage for moderating its foreign policy over the long term.

Mutual economic interests as well as common political goals facilitate Beijing-Seoul cooperation. The flow of investment, exports, and exchanges of students, tourists, and businessmen between China and South Korea has exploded in recent years. Bilateral trade between Seoul and Beijing reached $90 billion in 2004, a 42 percent increase from 2003, when China surpassed the United States as South Korea's largest trading partner.[221] Another reason Beijing has been cultivating relations with Seoul is to discourage South Koreans from developing overly close ties with Taiwan. In addition, by developing good economic and political relations with South Korea, Chinese policymakers hedge against the possibility that, at some point, South Korea will absorb North Korea without a major war (repeating Germany's experience in the 1990s). Maintaining good relations with Seoul could help limit Japanese and American influence in any newly reunited Korean state.

Russia's ties with South Korea have also improved considerably during the past decade. Like China, Russia and South Korea favor a "soft landing" for the DPRK regime—a gradual mellowing of its domestic and especially foreign policies, including the renunciation of nuclear weapons. Republic of Korea (ROK) President Roh Moo-hyun echoed Putin's observation that North Korea developed nuclear weapons in response to U.S. threats and to induce Washington to engage in a dialogue.[222] Such a benign outcome would circumvent all the feared consequences of precipitous regime change described above—humanitarian emergencies, economic reconstruction, arms races, and military conflicts. It would also allow for the continued growth of Russian-ROK commerce, which approximated $9 billion in 2006. The trade primarily involves the exchange of Russian oil and gas for South Korean machinery and equipment, but the ROK does purchase some Russian defense equipment. Since 1996, Russia has supplied tanks, combat vehicles, and military helicopters to the ROK military as partial payment of Russia's $2 billion debt to South Korea. The two governments plan to conduct joint naval exercises later this year.[223] Although not of paramount importance to either party, such bilateral ties provide both countries with leverage in their relations with other parties. From Moscow's perspective, they also help reaffirm Russia's status as an important country in East Asia after a period (the 1990s) when many observers questioned whether Moscow remained a regional player.

JAPAN

Japan's relations with both China and Russia remain troubled. Unlike the situation in Europe, the end of the Cold War has not brought about an equally dramatic improvement in the regional security environment of East Asia. In addition, whereas China and Russia have largely resolved their border disputes, their bilateral relations with Japan are each plagued by serious territorial conflicts. Nevertheless, Beijing and Moscow have both pursued their typically conflicted relations with Tokyo one-on-one, with no evident attempt to coordinate their postures regarding territorial disputes with Japan, or their anxieties over Japan's growing security role, or other issues.

China-Japan Relations.

Despite the recent upswing in their relationship, ties between China and Japan remain problematic. The two countries differ over each other's military modernization programs, access to natural resources under the East China Sea, and other important interests. More generally, the logic of great power rivalry encourages China to seek to weaken Japan's position, including its alliance with the United States. The Japanese, for their part, invariably worry about China's rising economic, political, and military power relative to that of Japan and its American ally. Both Tokyo and Beijing fear that Washington will move too far toward the other country. Russia's weaker position in East Asia has thus far distanced Moscow from these power calculations, but the Russian factor might change as it continues to strengthen economically and militarily and as China, Japan, and other Asian nations become increasingly dependent on Russian energy sources.[224]

Many Japanese businessmen continue to see China as a cornucopia of commercial opportunities. Sino-Japanese trade has surpassed U.S.-Japan trade, making China Japan's top trading partner even excluding goods and services exchanged via Hong Kong.[225] Yet, since the late 1990s, Chinese ships have conducted exploratory research within waters claimed by Japan, exacerbating their bilateral dispute over exploratory drilling rights in undersea natural gas fields in the East China Sea. Japan adheres to the UN Law of the Sea when defining its Exclusive Economic Zone (EEZ) as extending 200 miles from its shore. China asserts that its EEZ begins not at its coast, but from the edge of its submerged continental shelf. Recent Chinese drilling at the Chunxiao/Shirakaba gas fields and Japan's response have highlighted the dangers of these conflicting claims. Although the fields lie just inside China's side of the meridian separating the two countries' claims, Japanese experts believe that exploiting the fields would siphon gas from fields that extend under waters claimed by Japan—a situation disturbingly similar to that which Saddam Hussein cited to justify his invasion of Kuwait in 1990. In May 2004, Beijing authorized Chinese firms to commence exploratory drilling. In November 2004, the Japanese detected a Chinese *Han*-class nuclear submarine in its territorial waters near Taiwan.[226] Following a year of futile protests, Tokyo decided to permit Japanese firms to conduct their own explorations in the disputed region. After Chinese warships provocatively patrolled the area, the Japanese Coast Guard boldly assumed formal control over the contested Senkaku Islands south of Japan.[227] In November 2006 and January 2007, the Japanese government formally requested China to cease production at disputed gas fields in the East China Sea.[228]

With the end of the Soviet military threat, the Japanese have become increasingly concerned about China's military intentions and capabilities. Japanese policymakers have expressed particular concern about China's surging military spending, which has increased by double digits for many years, a level exceeding the country's average annual economic growth rate.[229] The Japan Defense Agency's security prospectus, titled *Defense of Japan 2005*, identified, for the first time, China's military modernization as potentially threatening and called on Beijing to make its defense programs more transparent.[230]

Since the late 1990s, the Chinese government has accelerated efforts to modernize and upgrade the PLA. China's lack of transparency regarding defense expenditures complicates intelligence estimates, but most foreign analysts calculate that, since the official Chinese budget figure of $36 billion excludes spending on military research and development, nuclear weapons, and major foreign weapons imports, actual PRC defense outlays total upwards of $60-90 billion annually.[231] The latest Chinese defense white paper outlines plans for an ambitious long-term effort to modernize all the branches of the PLA, from the army, navy, and air force to the Second Artillery Forces, which manage the country's strategic missile assets.[232] On March 4, 2007, the Chinese government announced one of its largest military spending increases in years, a 17.8 percent rise in its declared defense budget.[233]

Besides allowing the PRC to improve its traditionally weak indigenous defense industry, rapid economic growth has enabled China to become the world's largest arms importer. As discussed above, Russia has been an especially eager seller. China's recently acquired Russian weapons systems include advanced military aircraft (for example, Su-27s and Su-30), naval systems such as *Sovremenny*-class missile destroyers equipped with SS-N-22 *Sunburn* antiship missiles, and improved *Kilo*-class diesel attack submarines that would enhance the effectiveness of a Chinese military campaign against Taiwan. China is also devoting more resources to creating a domestic manufacturing process for advanced weapons systems. In late 2006, the PLA began deploying its first indigenously produced advanced jet fighter, the J-10, at bases across from Taiwan. China's space program has generated new surveillance, communication, and navigation satellites capable of supporting military operations against Taiwan and other contingencies external to the Chinese mainland.[234] As last year's events demonstrate, China has also developed ASAT capabilities. Overall, China's massive defense spending may be shifting the balance of power against Taiwan, making a coercive solution increasingly attractive to Beijing.[235]

Chinese-Japanese relations improved after Shinzo Abe became Japan's prime minister on September 26, 2006. His October 9, 2006, visit to Beijing ended an 18-month freeze on bilateral summits between the heads of the two governments. Before then, the Chinese government had frozen high-level summits with Japanese leaders outside the context of multilateral gatherings in order to protest the annual visits of Abe's predecessor, Junichiro Koizumi, to the Yasukuni Shrine. On November 19, China and Japan resumed their working-level defense dialogue, which had been in abeyance since March 2005. Chinese Premier Wen Jiabao's April 11-13, 2006, visit to Japan further advanced the modest détente that has marked Sino-Japanese relations. The two governments subsequently resumed military exchanges.[236]

Yet, the Chinese government's March 2007 announcement that it plans to increase its official defense budget, which foreign experts generally agree vastly understates the actual level of expenditures, to record levels has further deepened Japanese unease about Beijing's military buildup. At the time of Wen's visit, Japanese Defense Minster Fumio Kyuma acknowledged that China's expanding naval and air force capabilities also represented an issue of concern. Despite Beijing's protests, Abe continues to discourage European governments from ending their prohibition on arms sales to China.

At the April summit, the two countries agreed to create a hot line between their defense establishments. They also advanced plans to expand military exchanges, including reciprocal naval ship visits.[237] The communications link might help prevent the inadvertent escalation of future military incidents, such as would occur if the Japanese detect another Chinese submarine in their territorial waters. Neither the hot line nor the exchanges, however, will directly address the more general apprehension in Japan regarding China's long-term military plans and intentions.[238]

Russia-Japan Relations.

Relations between Russia and Japan remain equally problematic. Despite the end of the Cold War, the two countries have been unable to resolve their territorial dispute over what the Russians call the Southern Kurils and the Japanese label their Northern Territories. These islands—Kunashir (known in Japanese as Kunashiri), Iturup (Etorofu), Shikotan, and Habomai—have remained under Moscow's control since the Soviet military occupied them at the end of World War II. The Soviet government expelled the original inhabitants and established military bases and other settlements in their place. Japan has claimed that the San Francisco Treaty of 1951, under which it ceded over 50 Kuril islands to the Soviet Union, did not include the four islands comprising the Northern Territories.[239] A 1956 Joint Declaration restored diplomatic ties between Russia and Japan, but the dispute has prevented their signing a formal peace treaty. Various proposals to divide control of the islands or establish a creative shared-sovereignty arrangement have never gained decisive support in both governments simultaneously.[240]

In 1993, when Boris Yeltsin visited Japan, expectations were high that bilateral relations would improve, as they had done with Russia's western neighbors. The two governments signed the Tokyo Declaration which called for closer Russia-Japan cooperation. Although a dispute soon arose regarding the disposal of Russian nuclear waste in the Sea of Japan, in 1995 the two countries initiated cooperation in building suitable nuclear waste processing facilities, including a nuclear waste ship financed by Russia, Japan, and the United States.[241] The Japanese government subsequently provided Russia with financial and other assistance for disposal of antiquated nuclear-powered submarines which contained spent radioactive fuel and other radioactive waste.[242]

For various reasons, this limited security cooperation failed to expand into a more comprehensive rapprochement between the two countries. In addition to the sovereignty dispute, the two sides have criticized each other's defense cooperation with third parties. The Japanese have complained that Russia's vast military sales to China were enhancing the ability of the Chinese military to project power against Taiwan and potentially Japan. For their part, the Russian officials have repeatedly objected to the growing U.S.-Japanese cooperation on constructing ballistic missile defenses.

The sovereignty dispute has also engendered recurring mutual recriminations about alleged territorial violations. Russian ships regularly detain Japanese sailors who attempt to fish in the waters surrounding the disputed islands, charging them with violating Russia's maritime boundaries. In August 2007, a Russian coast guard ship killed a crew member of a Japanese fishing boat with a warning shot aimed at the vessel.[243] In turn, the Japanese government has alleged that Russian military aircraft have periodically violated Japan's air space. The most recent incident occurred in early February, when a Russian *Tupolev* Tu-95 bomber, ignoring the warnings of the Japanese fighter aircraft sent to intercept it, overflew the uninhabited island of Sofugan in the Izu island chain south of Tokyo during a February 2008 Pacific Ocean exercise.[244] Japanese authorities have also recently accused Russian diplomats of spying on members of the Japanese cabinet.[245] Although Russian representatives denied both accusations, Japanese nationalists used the espionage incident as a convenient excuse to resume denouncing Moscow for allegedly pursuing hostile policies towards Japan.[246]

Economic relations between Russia and Japan have largely stagnated, despite the exploding commerce elsewhere in the Asia Pacific region and despite a seemingly natural partnership emerging between the Russians, who desire Japanese financial and other assistance in developing eastern Russia, and the Japanese, who seek to purchase Russian energy exports. Preoccupation with the territorial dispute overshadowed Putin's September 2000 visit to Japan, notwithstanding hopes that the two governments could somehow set aside the issue while concentrating on strengthening economic ties. In 2003, Koizumi and Putin signed a number of documents aimed at improving bilateral commercial relations.[247] Yet, the chaotic economic conditions in Russia under Yeltsin and the predatory state capitalist policies pursued by the Putin administration have done little to encourage Japanese investment in Russia, particularly when enticing opportunities already exist in China, the United States, and other regions. In addition, the Russians have hesitated about antagonizing Beijing by committing to supply Japan with the energy supplies also coveted by Chinese energy importers. Chinese policymakers have done nothing to encourage an enduring Russian-Japanese reconciliation, while preoccupied American leaders have seemingly neglected the issue.

TAIWAN

Russia has taken care to ensure that its relations with Taiwan remain correct but profitable. During the Cold War, Taiwan refused to establish any official contact with communist countries. Even after the emergence of the Sino-Soviet split, Taiwanese authorities still prohibited direct trade with the USSR, whose government continued to adhere to a "One China Policy." It was only during the 1980s that commerce began to develop between the two countries.[248]

After the end of the Cold War, Taipei sought to develop better relations with Russia's newly emergent noncommunist government. In October 1990, Moscow Mayor Gavriil Kharitonovich Popov visited Taiwan, the first Russian official to visit Taiwan since World War II.[249] In 1992, the two countries established a Taipei-Moscow Coordination Commission on Economic and Cultural Cooperation. The commission is a de facto equivalent to the Taipei Representative Offices in other countries that formally recognize Beijing as the legitimate authority over the whole of China. The Russian government established a similar office in Taipei in 1996. By 1994, trade between them had reached $1 billion, which was 7.7 times higher than that of 1986.[250] In 2002, the Taipei-Russia Association was established in Taipei as a nonprofit organization to facilitate cooperation between the two governments.

Taiwan is Russia's fourth biggest trading partner in the Asian-Pacific region. Unlike its trade with China, Russia enjoys a positive balance in trading with Taiwan. Taipei is content with this imbalance because Russian raw materials are often cheaper than those from other sources. In 2003, Taiwan began importing oil from Russia's Sakhalin energy complex. Russia and Taiwan continue to discuss expanding this energy trade. Taiwanese officials also hope that their country's extensive commercial ties with Russia will induce Moscow to use its good offices to discourage Beijing from adopting disruptive policies toward Taiwan. Cultural exchanges involving artists, athletes, tourists, and students have also flourished between Russia and Taiwan.

Yet, Russia has been treading the line very carefully in dealing with Taipei in order to avoid upsetting Beijing. Russian government representatives have deliberately separated their economic and cultural intercourse with Taiwan from official political ties.[251] Yeltsin's 1992 Executive Order on Russian-Taiwanese relations, which prohibits interaction beyond personal and nonofficial encounters, is still the guiding principle in Russia's Taiwan policy.

This principle has been reaffirmed in the numerous declarations issued whenever the two governments have conducted joint meetings as well as in the 2001 Treaty of Good-Neighborliness and Friendly Cooperation. On July 23, 2007, for instance, Russian Deputy Foreign Minister Alexander Yakovenko, in meetings with a visiting Chinese diplomatic delegation, criticized the efforts of the Taiwanese government to seek international recognition of its independence by pursuing membership in the UN as an independent country. In its report on the encounter, the Russian

Foreign Ministry stated that "it was confirmed during the meeting that Russia is against any possible form of Taiwan's independence, recognizing only one China, and the government of the Chinese People's Republic as the only legitimate government representing China."[252] Russia has continued its extensive arms sales to Beijing, heedless of Taiwanese complaints that such sales threaten Taiwan by encouraging Beijing to contemplate military options in resolving the Beijing-Taipei dispute.

SOUTH ASIA

The limits of foreign policy harmonization between China and Russia are also visible in South Asia, where the two governments have adopted sharply divergent positions on important issues. For instance, despite the recent improvement in Chinese-Indian relations, Russia's ties with New Delhi still remain much stronger than those between China and India. Persistent border disputes, differences over India's growing security ties with the United States, competition over energy supplies, and other sources of Sino-Indian tensions have consistently impeded realization of the vision of a Moscow-Beijing-New Delhi axis that has periodically surfaced over the past decade (recall especially the endorsement of such an axis expressed by former Russian Prime Minister Yevgeny Primakov during a visit to New Delhi in 1998).

Until recently, relations between China and India were visibly strained. The two countries fought a short border war in 1962 and have never resolved their conflicting claims. During the Cold War, India was in a de facto alliance with the Soviet Union against China. Beijing has long cultivated close ties with India's arch rival, Pakistan. China provided the Pakistanis with military equipment and technology, and helped them develop nuclear weapons and ballistic missiles that target India. When India tested a nuclear weapon in May 1998, Defense Minister George Fernandes justified this controversial action by citing China's military ties with Pakistan.[253]

Relations among the three great Asian powers have stabilized since the Cold War. Along with Brazil, the three countries are considered core members of BRIC, the widely used acronym for the world's most important emerging economies—Brazil, Russia, India, and China. India also enjoys permanent observer status in the SCO, the most influential multinational organization linking China and Russia. The three countries also rank among the world's most populous nations, with China and India together home to over one-third of humanity. Commercial ties between the three countries have grown substantially in recent years, albeit from low levels and despite persistent Russian and Indian complaints about enduring trade imbalances with their economically booming rival.

The improvement in Sino-Indian ties is particularly noteworthy. The two countries' prime ministers and other senior government officials have engaged in a wide-ranging dialogue that encompasses many economic, energy, security, and cultural issues. As part of these exchanges, in late May 2006 the two countries' defense ministers signed their first Memorandum of Understanding on Defense Cooperation. The accord provides for frequent meetings between civilian and military members of their defense communities as well as further joint military exercises and training in areas of mutual interest.[254] In 2005, China and India declared that, despite their continuing disagreements, their policies would reflect a shared commitment to establish a bilateral "strategic partnership."

Bilateral Sino-Indian commerce has also increased to a point where, in 2004, China became India's second-largest trading partner, behind only the United States. In March 2006, Beijing proposed a bilateral free trade agreement that could result in China's replacing the United States as India's largest trading partner by 2012.[255] Chinese and Indian officials also committed their governments to expanding cooperation in agriculture, information technologies, and other sectors. Russian government representatives have encouraged this reduction in Sino-Indian tensions, which have complicated Moscow's Asian diplomacy for decades.[256] Nevertheless, efforts to form a trilateral bloc among Beijing, Moscow, and New Delhi have repeatedly foundered on these same persistent Sino-Indian tensions.

Although Chinese and Indians have long sought to overcome their lingering border dispute, since June 2003 their Special Representatives have achieved only modest progress notwithstanding the 11 formal rounds of negotiations they have held on the issue. The April 2005 Sino-Indian agreement merely establishes the basic *principles* that their negotiators should consider in crafting a framework for resolving the dispute rather than specifying the precise *terms* for a future settlement. In a commentary on Manmohan Singh's January 2008 visit to Beijing, the first visit by an Indian Prime Minister to China in 5 years, the Chinese state-owned news media cautioned that "settlement of the issue will depend on wisdom, vision, and flexibility. It is unrealistic to expect a solution from a single meeting," a formulation obscuring the fact that the boundary question had been under active negotiation for years.[257]

The two governments also continue to differ on India's aspiration to become a permanent member of the UNSC. The text of the joint vision declaration issued by the Indian and Chinese prime ministers states simply that "the Indian side reiterates its aspirations for permanent membership of the UN Security Council." It fails to include a corresponding Chinese endorsement, content merely with this formulation: "The Chinese side understands and supports India's aspirations to play a greater role in the United Nations, including in the Security Council."[258] Reading between the lines, we infer that Beijing evidently still seeks to preserve its unique status as one of the five veto-wielding members on the Security Council, and the only permanent member from East Asia. Among other considerations, keeping Japan off the Council would become harder if India were to join.

The Chinese are also aware that their cities are the targets of India's ever longer-range ballistic missiles. The Indians in turn understand that the Chinese are unenthusiastic about the recent strengthening of Indian-American and Indian-Japanese security ties.[259] During the second Clinton administration, U.S. Deputy Secretary of State Strobe Talbott and Indian Foreign Minister Jaswant Singh engaged in wide-ranging discussions about regional security issues.[260] Under the George W. Bush administration, both countries have pursued expanded cooperation on a "quartet" of issues under the initiative known as the "Next Steps in Strategic Partnership" (NSSP). The NSSP, launched in January 2004, encompasses joint efforts to expand collaboration on high-technology trade, outer space exploration, ballistic missile defense, and civilian nuclear power. In addition, the Indian government has begun purchasing more American weapons systems to complement its predominately Russian-made and indigenously manufactured defense equipment. One of the factors encouraging Indian-American security cooperation has been their shared concern over China's growing economic and military power. In the view of many strategists, India and the United States share a common interest in curbing Chinese efforts to expand its influence in Bangladesh, Myanmar, and the South China Sea as part of a "string of pearls" strategy.[261]

The Chinese government has yet to endorse the proposed U.S.-Indian civil nuclear energy cooperation agreement announced in a July 2005 joint statement between U.S. President George Bush and Prime Minister Manmohan Singh. The Henry J. Hyde United States-India Peaceful Atomic Energy Cooperation Act would grant India unprecedented exemptions in American law and global export rules in exchange for India's opening its civilian nuclear power plants to international inspection. The 45-nation Nuclear Suppliers Group, which operates by consensus, is scheduled to vote later this year on whether to permit New Delhi to import nuclear material and technology despite India's refusal to accede to the Nuclear Nonproliferation Treaty (NPT). When President Hu Jintao visited India in November 2006, both governments agreed in principle to cooperate on peaceful nuclear energy, but concrete projects have yet to emerge. Chinese and Indian firms also compete for oil and gas supplies in Central Asia, Africa, and other regions.[262]

In addition, Chinese policymakers have become uneasy about the growing security cooperation between New Delhi and Tokyo. Japanese policymakers have described India as an important international partner, given the two countries' common democratic political systems and their shared concerns about keeping China's rise peaceful. Beijing clearly desires to avoid engaging in direct confrontations with New Delhi for fear that it will only intensify U.S.-Indian security cooperation. Nevertheless, the Chinese government continues to tilt toward Pakistan in that country's disputes with India.[263]

THE MIDDLE EAST

The governments of China and Russia have pursued parallel but typically uncoordinated policies in the Middle East. They both want to sell Iran weapons and other items, and have defended Tehran in the Security Council even while warning against any Iranian ambitions to acquire nuclear weapons. In addition, they both opposed the U.S.-led invasion of Iraq but are concerned that an early American military withdrawal from that country could lead to an increase of Islamic militarism throughout the Middle East, which could disrupt China's energy supplies and reinvigorate the Muslim insurgency in southern Russia. Thus far, however, neither country has sought to make the issue a major point of confrontation with Washington.

Iran.

The protracted tensions between Tehran and the West have led to the emergence of a distinct "Asia Look" philosophy in Iran that would break with Iran's traditional westward orientation. Instead, the Asia Look philosophy envisages Iran as a Eurasian country whose natural partners include China, Russia, and other Asian countries.[264] Despite their different official religious inclinations and natural resource endowments, the incumbent governments of China, Russia, and Iran share important interests in Eurasia. The most important of these include promoting the region's energy and economic development as an alternative to Western markets, countering Sunni-inspired terrorism, and balancing Western influence in general.[265]

When the Soviet Union disintegrated in the early 1990s, the Iranian government resisted any temptation to conduct an extensive campaign of Islamic proselytization in the newly independent Central Asian republics.[266] Instead, Iranian officials have respected Russia's primacy when dealing with internal dynamics of Central Asian countries.[267] For example, Tehran endorsed Russia's military intervention during the Tajikistan civil war. Iran's bilateral ties with Russia remain more important than its still limited relations with the Central Asian states.

Furthermore, since Iran hopes to expand its commercial relations with Central Asia, and fears the arrival of another civil war such as that in Afghanistan, which flooded Iran with millions of refugees, Tehran views Russia's stabilizing military presence with favor. The Russian government has reciprocated by supporting Iran's observer status in the SCO and by promoting its economic integration into the region. After meeting with President Mahmoud Ahmadinejad at the June 2006 SCO summit in Shanghai, Putin told reporters that Gazprom was prepared to participate in the proposed Iran-Pakistan-India natural gas pipeline despite American opposition. He also announced Russia's interest in creating a joint venture with Iran to exploit both countries' natural gas reserves.[268]

Russian and Iranian officials have been some of the strongest advocates of establishing an "energy club" among Eurasian countries. At the June 2006 Shanghai summit, Ahmadinejad invited the other SCO member governments to discussions in Iran "to explore more effective ways of co-operating in the exploration, exploitation, transport, and conversion of energy."[269] At the August 2007 SCO summit, Ahmadinejad reaffirmed Tehran's interest in helping the SCO to create a regional energy grouping, repeating his offer to host a meeting of oil and gas policymakers from SCO members to "optimize cooperation in transportation, prospecting, development, and refining."[270]

Iran also welcomes the growing presence of China, another status quo power, in its region. Iran's ties with China encompass both the defense sector and civilian commerce, especially energy.[271] The volume of Chinese-Iranian trade jumped 70 percent between 2005 and 2006, to $3.2 billion.[272] Iran has become one of China's most critical oil suppliers, while Chinese companies provide Iran with important industrial technologies and specialty metals as well as diverse commercial products. For several years, the two governments have been seeking to finalize a multi-billion dollar energy deal that could see Sinopec, China's largest refiner, purchasing 250 million tons of liquefied natural gas over a 25-year period.[273]

Iranian efforts to acquire sensitive nuclear technologies, such as the capacity to enrich uranium to manufacture nuclear fuel, have been the main factor complicating its relations with Moscow and Beijing. Since the National Council of Resistance of Iran revealed the existence of clandestine Iranian nuclear activities at the enrichment facility at Natanz and the heavy water plant at Arak in August 2002, the international community has been pressing the Iranian government to clarify the status of its nuclear research program. After inspectors from the International Atomic Energy Agency (IAEA) found evidence of additional secret Iranian nuclear programs, including some with possible military applications, the IAEA declared in June 2003 that Iran had violated its commitments under the NPT to provide comprehensive reports on its nuclear material and nuclear-related activities. In September 2005, the IAEA Board of Governors formally found Tehran in noncompliance with its NPT safeguards agreement. In December 2006 and March 2007, the UNSC imposed sanctions on the Iranian government in a thus far unsuccessful attempt to coerce Iran into ending its uranium enrichment activities.

Throughout this process, the Chinese and Russian governments have been reluctant supporters of punitive measures. Chinese and Russian diplomats often worked to soften proposed sanctions. In addition, they have always defended Iran's right to pursue nuclear activities for peaceful purposes such as civilian energy production. In a joint declaration issued during the March 2007 Hu-Putin summit, China and Russia reaffirmed that Iran had the right to pursue civilian nuclear energy if it adhered to the provisions of the Nuclear NPT. They also insisted that the dispute over Iran's nuclear program had to be settled through peaceful means.[274] Russian officials have also been particularly adamant in denying that the Iranian government is currently seeking a nuclear weapon or is developing the long-range missile technology that NATO governments have cited to justify deploying ballistic missile defense in Poland and the Czech Republic. At the 2007 SCO summit, Lavrov repeated the longstanding Russian position that, according to "the quite precise information at our disposal, we can see no such long-term threat."[275]

Nevertheless, there has been considerable evidence of renewed Russian-Iranian tensions over Tehran's nuclear ambitions. In early August 2007, European officials told the news media that the Russian government had informed Iran in July that Moscow would refuse to supply nuclear fuel for the Russian-built nuclear reactor in Bushehr until Tehran provided more details about its past nuclear activities to the international community. The Russian Foreign Ministry declined to confirm the report, but did acknowledge that various problems would delay the fuel shipments.[276]

Putin's offer during the June 2007 G-8 summit in Germany to permit the U.S. military to use the Russian-leased early warning radar at Gabala, Azerbaijan, for monitoring Iran's missile development program has also intensified Iranian fears that Moscow would sacrifice Iranian interests when they conflict with other Russian strategic priorities. After Putin first made the Gabala offer, Kazern Jalali, a member of the Iranian parliament and rapporteur of the Majlis National Security and Foreign Policy Committee, complained that the Russian government should not treat Iran as a "tool" for resolving great power disputes.[277]

Although Russia began shipping uranium fuel to Iran's Bushehr reactor on December 17, 2007, Russian and Iranian leaders continue to disagree as to whether Iran should continue developing its own capacity to enrich nuclear fuel, which would also provide the wherewithal to manufacture nuclear weapons. On December 26, the Russian Foreign Minister said that the deliveries meant that Iran had no logical economic reasons to make its own fuel since Russian suppliers could provide it, obviating Iran's plan to construct its own costly nuclear enrichment, storage, and reprocessing facilities. Even the December 2007 U.S. National Intelligence Estimate, which concluded that Iran had abandoned its nuclear weapons program in 2003 and led Lavrov to repeat that Russian intelligence had no evidence that Iran had been pursuing nuclear weapons even before 2003, has not softened Russian objections to Iran's uranium enrichment program.

Iranian officials have complained for years over delays at the construction site at Bushehr. Russian officials have cited payment delays from Iranian customers, problems of integrating the original and now outdated German equipment with Russian technologies, and other logistical/technological difficulties. Although Russia has begun delivering nuclear fuel to Bushehr, Russians involved in the project claim that the soonest the plant could begin operating would be in late 2008. In December 2007, Irina Yesipova, a spokesperson for Atomstroiexport, estimated that Bushehr could not begin producing commercial power for another year. Iranian representatives have dismissed such difficulties, suggesting that Moscow has been deliberately prevaricating in order to avoid antagonizing Western governments that object to the project.

During his October 2007 visit to Tehran, Lavrov reaffirmed Moscow's opposition to imposing any additional sanctions against Iran without the specific approval of the UNSC, where Russia enjoys the right of veto. In his meetings with Iranian President Mahmoud Ahmadinejad and Iranian Foreign Minister Manouchehr Motaki, Lavrov urged Tehran to cooperate with the IAEA in clarifying unresolved questions concerning Iran's nuclear program. At the same time, Lavrov defended Iran's right to undertake a peaceful nuclear energy program provided that it adhered to the provisions of the Nuclear NPT and related international agreements.

That same month, Russian President Putin told a nationwide television telephone call-in audience that threats and pressure only reinforced Iranian leaders' determination to acquire nuclear weapons to bolster their security. Putin told one caller that "direct contact between the leaders of countries that are encountering problems is always more productive and a quicker road to success than a policy of threats, sanctions, and even more so using the pressure of force."[278] Putin formulated Moscow's position as follows: "We have no evidence of Iran's intention to produce nuclear weapons. Therefore, we proceed from the premise that Iran has no such plans. But we share the concern of other partners and believe that Iran's programs must be transparent." Whereas U.S. and Israeli officials would like to see a regime change in Tehran, Russian leaders want changes in Iranian policies but not a change in the regime itself.[279] In any case, Russian firms continued to fulfill their lucrative 1995 contract to resume construction of the nuclear reactor at Bushehr despite American protests. In early 2008, Russia shipped the uranium fuel to Iran for use at the reactor when construction is completed.

Russian officials have had to balance a complex set of objectives in their relations with Tehran. They desire Iranian help in curbing international terrorism, especially in the former Soviet republics neighboring Russia, and in limiting American influence in Central Asia and the Middle East. Russian nuclear and defense firms also profit from Iran's dependence on Russian-made nuclear technology and weapons. Nevertheless, Russian leaders oppose Iran's development of nuclear weapons. Their opposition is apparently due less to concern about a near-term Iranian threat to Russia than to fears of how Israel, the United States, and European governments might respond to an Iranian atomic bomb program. A major new conflict in the Persian Gulf could lead to further upward ratcheting of world prices for oil and gas, generating windfall profits for Moscow. But Russian territory lies uncomfortably close to the site of any Persian Gulf military operation. Another war could also encourage Islamist extremism throughout the area or lead to regime change in Iran, with unpredictable consequences.

Nevertheless, though Russian policymakers consider preventing Iran from developing the capacity to manufacture nuclear weapons to be exceptionally important, other influential Russians apparently place a higher priority on pursuing a number of hoped-for arms deals with Iran. Moscow hopes that Tehran will buy more advanced Russian weapons systems and Russian nuclear technology. Between 2002 and 2005, the Iranian military purchased approximately $1.7 billion worth of Russian weapons. The Russian government is reportedly negotiating the sale of 250 Su-30 *Flanker* fighter-bombers to Iran in a deal that could bring another $1 billion into Russian coffers. The recent announcement of a major U.S. arms deal with Iran's Persian Gulf neighbors, which would divert money that might otherwise have gone to purchase Russian arms, may reinforce Moscow's interest in remaining Iran's major weapons supplier.

The Russian government also needs Iran's endorsement of any multinational regime for exploiting the energy riches of the Caspian Sea. The littoral countries remain engaged in negotiations over an acceptable legal framework for governing how they can extract its valuable natural resources. Current estimates indicate that the Caspian Sea contains the world's third-largest reserves of oil and natural gas, as well as considerable quantities of sturgeon and other fish.[280] At present, the littoral countries remain divided over whether to classify the Caspian as a sea or an inland lake. If the littoral states were to treat the Caspian as a sea, then each country would control the territorial waters along their coasts, leaving Kazakhstan and Russia with the largest and potentially most lucrative shares. If the Caspian were treated legally as a large inland lake, all the littoral states could share equally in its natural resources or agree on some other arrangement. In 2003, Azerbaijan, Kazakhstan, and Russia reached a trilateral agreement that divided the northern 64 percent of the Caspian Sea into three unequal shares. Iran and Turkmenistan, however, refused to endorse this trilateral agreement and continue to claim larger economic zones than the 2003 formula would provide.

In the past, American officials have criticized Russia and China for maintaining extensive commercial relations with Iran despite Tehran's pursuit of sensitive nuclear technologies, its ties to foreign terrorist movements, and its anti-Western and anti-Israeli rhetoric. Recent U.S. efforts have focused on securing Moscow's and Beijing's support for limited international sanctions aimed at preventing Iran from developing an independent capacity to manufacture nuclear fuel through uranium enrichment, a technology that also can be used to make nuclear bombs. American efforts in this regard have included diplomatic engagement with the Chinese and Russian governments as well as the imposition of unilateral economic sanctions against Chinese and Russian firms that have provided Iran with equipment or technologies that can be used to build WMD or the means to deliver them (e.g., ballistic missiles). Since 2005, the United States has imposed sanctions on nine Chinese companies believed to have shipped restricted items to Iran, perhaps without the authorization of the Chinese government, whose new export controls often prohibit such transactions.[281] The U.S. penalties typically include barring these firms from doing business with the U.S. Government or American companies.

Iraq.

Chinese and Russian officials argued against the launch of Operation IRAQI FREEDOM, but their opposition manifested itself less visibly than that of many other governments, including some long-standing American allies. Furthermore, Beijing and Moscow have declined to make the issue a priority in their relations, either with Washington or with each other. Chinese and Russian leaders simply joined international calls for an immediate cessation of hostilities during the invasion and, after the fighting ended, urged a greater role for the UN during the subsequent occupation.

In March 2003, Putin criticized the U.S. decision to invade Iraq, telling senior ministers in the Kremlin: "Military action can in no way be justified. Military action is a big political error."[282] At the time, however, Putin and other Russians might have feared that a quick and successful U.S. intervention in Iraq would establish a pro-American government there and might negatively affect Russia's economic interests, especially since Moscow had secured several lucrative commercial deals with Saddam Hussein's regime. Ironically, the invasion might have actually helped the Russian economy by contributing to surging world oil prices.

Putin and other Russian leaders have nevertheless called on the United States and other foreign troops to withdraw from Iraq as soon as possible and grant the UN a prominent role in its restoration. Lavrov has claimed that "Iraq is our common problem which has to be tackled by joint efforts of all the parties concerned."[283]

The Chinese government also actively opposed the American-led military intervention in Iraq in 2003. Although Chinese government representatives objected that the operation violated international law, strategic and economic considerations appear to have played a greater part in determining Beijing's response. Some Chinese strategists feared that the occupation of yet another nearby country by U.S. troops would facilitate any U.S. effort to encircle China. Perhaps even more important were Beijing's concerns about the negative commercial consequences. China had developed substantial economic interests with Saddam Hussein's regime. Before the war, Chinese firms had actively pursued oil and construction contracts with Iraq under the UN Oil-for-Food program. China feared that a war in Iraq would substantially hurt Chinese interests since it would result in the loss of Iraqi contracts valued at over $1 billion, as well as potentially disrupt Chinese oil supplies and raise oil prices.[284]

Nevertheless, China's Iraq policy since 2003 has deliberately sought to avoid a confrontation with the United States over Iraq. In February 2003, the Chinese government declined to sign on to the joint French-Russian-German statement criticizing the invasion. In June 2004, China voted for Security Council Resolution 1546, which legitimized the presence of the U.S.-led multinational force in Iraq.[285] In June 2007, the Chinese delegation voted to extend that mandate.[286] Moreover, official Chinese criticism of U.S. Iraq policy has been consistently mild. After the late 2006 release of the report of the Iraq Study Group, Chinese Foreign Ministry spokesperson Qin Gang declared that "China hopes to see a stabilized Iraq governed by its people, who can enjoy a peaceful and stable life as soon as possible. We also hope that the Iraq issue be handled properly in compliance with relevant resolutions adopted by the UN Security Council."[287]

Like Russia, the Chinese government has consistently sought to expand the role of the UN in Iraq.[288] Since both Beijing and Moscow enjoy veto power in the UNSC, they could use the institution to constrain American influence in the region as well as enhance their own leverage in dealing with the Iraqi authorities. In addition, by consistently publicly affirming the need to respect Iraqi sovereignty and give the international community a larger role in Iraqi affairs, Chinese and Russian representatives may hope to gain favor with Arabs and Muslims.[289]

Some Chinese and Russians also perceive the conflict as an opportunity for commercial profit. Chinese arms dealers have sold weapons both to the Iraqi government and, allegedly, to the anti-government insurgents that are fighting American troops. Foreign experts continue to disagree over the extent to which Chinese officials endorse or are even aware of arms sales to the insurgents, which appear to be flowing through Iran.[290] American officials have downplayed the issue of culpability and simply called on the Chinese governments to "do a better job of policing these sales."[291] The Chinese Foreign Ministry issued a statement insisting that the Chinese government never sold arms to "non-country entities or people" because it "takes a scrupulous and responsible attitude to the export of its arms," a formulation that conveniently ignored the issue of transfers from Iran or by nongovernmental Chinese entities.[292] Chinese Foreign Ministry representatives have also maintained that their companies should be permitted to participate in Iraqi reconstruction projects, and have forgiven past Iraqi government debt to China in order to be able to do so.[293]

Russian officials have also not overlooked opportunities for financial gain from the conflict. In April 2007, the Russian government launched a sustained campaign in support of Lukoil's bid to develop a major Iraqi oil field in West Qurna.[294] Lukoil is Russia's largest oil company, and the West Qurna oil reserves are believed to be some of the world's largest, with a potential of around four billion barrels. Kremlin spokesman Dmitry Peskov said:

> Defending the interests of Russian companies abroad as a whole is a matter of importance for the government . . . and it is also an important priority for the president. As far as Lukoil is concerned, it is a major company that is expanding its reach in many countries of the world. . . . The intentions of the company to expand its presence in Iraq is supported in Russia.[295]

Both the Chinese and Russian governments have offered to write off almost all of Iraq's Saddam-era debt in return for Baghdad's agreeing to reconsider some Saddam-era energy projects that would see Chinese and Russian companies develop major Iraqi oil fields.[296]

The inability of the United States thus far to achieve a stable, allied Iraqi government is a mixed blessing for Chinese and Russian interests in Iraq and the Middle East. On the one hand, Beijing and Moscow potentially benefit from any resurgence of American isolationism induced by defeat in Iraq, since it would open the door for them to displace U.S. influence in the area. More generally, Chinese and Russian leaders would see any U.S. military defeat as a welcome sign that America's global security primacy was on the wane.

On the other hand, chaos in Iraq that infected the neighboring countries of Kuwait, Iran, and Saudi Arabia could threaten the security of China's energy suppliers from the Persian Gulf. For this reason, some Chinese energy experts have called for the international community to work with the United States to help stabilize the situation in Iraq.[297]

Russian analysts seem even more aware of this problem. In June 2006 the Mujahideen Shura Council in Iraq kidnapped several Russian diplomats in Baghdad. Despite their ongoing insurgency in Iraq, the radical Islamists still found time to express their solidarity with Chechen Muslims. The kidnappers demanded that Moscow pull its troops out of Chechnya within 48 hours and executed the hostages when Moscow did not comply.[298] Likewise, in January 2007, the Russian embassy in Baghdad was sprayed with gunfire. Following the attack, Russia's Foreign Ministry released a statement claiming that "Russia firmly demands from Iraqi authorities that they urgently undertake all necessary steps to strengthen the system of physical protection of our diplomatic mission." The ministry also made it clear that it held the United States jointly responsible for the security of diplomatic missions in Iraq.[299]

These episodes have underscored to Russian policymakers the risks of a terrorist takeover of Iraq should the United States withdraw its forces from the country prematurely. Reflecting this concern, Maksim Yusin, a political analyst on the staff of *Izvestia*, wrote in March 2007:

> Better the current puppet government in Baghdad than al-Qaida, which would almost certainly gain control over several Iraqi provinces once the Americans were to "distance themselves." Then die-hard "jihadists" would pour into Iraq from other regions, including the North Caucasus . . . and the jihadists would start dashing back and forth like shuttle merchants—off to Russia to blow something up, then back to Iraq for R&R. . . . So it would be better if the Americans would just stay put.[300]

In June 2007, Russia backed the UNSC resolution that extended the mandate for the U.S.-led Multinational Force in Iraq and urged the international community to support Iraq in its pursuit of national reconciliation and economic development.[301] Russian Foreign Minister Lavrov stated that while it is impossible to stabilize Iraq with military force alone, it is essential that reconciliation in that country be reached with the help of all the parties concerned. For its part, "Russia is ready to continue participating actively in efforts to promote just this approach."[302] The problem that now exists for Moscow is that while a strong American presence in the Middle East limits Russian influence in the region, a weak American presence may threaten Russian influence even more.[303]

CONCLUSION AND POLICY RECOMMENDATIONS

Although Chinese-Russian relations have improved along several important dimensions, security cooperation between China and Russia has remained tenuous. The two governments support each other on some issues but differ on others, as might be expected from an opportunistic relationship in which both countries following their own interests. Since these interests conflict as well as coincide, the relationship is not necessarily moving in an anti-American direction. But since nothing these two great powers do on the world stage is insignificant, Washington must continue to monitor carefully developments in Beijing and Moscow. Thus far, their fitfully improving relationship has not presented a major security challenge to the United States or its allies.

Nevertheless, modern history has witnessed major transformations in ties between Beijing and Moscow that affected U.S. security—from allies in the 1950s to armed adversaries in the 1960s. It thus behooves American national security planners to anticipate the potential for major discontinuities in Sino-Russian relations. Above all, American officials need to pursue a mixture of shaping and hedging policies that aim to avert the advent of a hostile Chinese-Russian alignment while concurrently preparing the United States to better counter such a development should it arise.

The U.S. Government should therefore pursue several policies designed to prevent Russia and China from developing a genuine strategic alliance, which could impede the attainment of important American foreign policy goals. Although the probability of such a bloc is low, the negative consequences for U.S. policies in East Asia and elsewhere could be quite severe should one emerge. Washington also needs to hedge against the possibility that unanticipated factors beyond its control will engender such an anti-American coalition.

Continued efforts to maintain strong U.S.-European and U.S.-Japanese security ties represent an essential hedging strategy against the emergence of a hostile Chinese-Russian military bloc. The transatlantic and U.S.-Japanese alliances, unlike the weaker Sino-Russian alignment, involve extensive cooperation, and not only in the military sphere. More generally, U.S. officials should continue to retain robust military forces in the European and Asian-Pacific regions. Reductions in the size of the U.S. military presence on the European continent and in the western Pacific could prove possible or even necessary, but they should proceed in a deliberate manner and in close consultation with other governments. Regardless of the numbers involved, the military presence reassures these countries about the value of maintaining good relations with the United States. The possibility that many governments neighboring China and Russia would side with Washington against a Sino-Russian bloc presumably deters these two governments from seeking one.

In this regard, the United States will continue to benefit from underlying regional anxieties about the implications of the continuing growth of Chinese and Russian military strength in recent years. At a minimum, Europeans and Asians would want to sustain ties with the United States in order to enjoy some negotiating leverage with Beijing and Moscow. Concerns about the reversal under Putin of many previously liberalized Russian foreign and defense policies and the longer-term growth of Chinese military power should help sustain regional support for keeping a robust U.S. military presence in Europe and Asia.[304] A strengthening of Russia-Chinese defense links, perhaps within a SCO framework, could lead their neighbors to seek balance by moving even closer to Washington. Reassuring these governments that the United States is willing and capable of protecting their interests also helps dampen incentives for horizontal nuclear proliferation in those regions.[305]

U.S. policymakers should also continue to encourage reconciliation between Russia and Japan. Better ties between Moscow and Tokyo would give Moscow an alternative to aligning with China on Asian security issues. Furthermore, stronger commercial ties between Moscow and Tokyo could improve the prospects that the two countries will resolve the Kurile Islands dispute, perhaps through some creative shared-sovereignty arrangement. The United States also has an interest in dampening differences between Japan and China. The accelerated development of the undersea energy resources in the Pacific Ocean would enhance the ability of all three countries to hedge against future disruptions of Persian Gulf oil supplies. The stubbornly persisting dispute between China and Japan over the two countries' contested maritime claims has impeded progress on this issue. American policies can help moderate tensions by encouraging Chinese and Japanese leaders to focus on current opportunities—such as the development of the gas fields located in their disputed waters—rather than past differences.

The need to respond to North Korea's nuclear program has created opportunities for improved U.S. and Japanese relations with China. Perhaps the most important difference between the 1994 Agreed Framework and the February 2007 denuclearization accord is the Chinese government's far greater support of the 2007 settlement. From Beijing's perspective, a successful outcome to the Six-Party process would both eliminate the problems that a North Korean nuclear arsenal would present for China and help reinforce perceptions of Beijing as a committed and influential regional security stakeholder.

Similarly, Russian and American leaders have cited their cooperation in managing the North Korean nuclear dispute as demonstrating that the two governments can continue to work together in resolving important international security issues, despite their many bilateral differences.[306] A future source of Sino-Russian tension might be how Beijing and Moscow respond to the U.S. position that the main players in any comprehensive peace settlement to replace the 1953 Korean War armistice should be confined to the two Koreas, China, and the United States. Such a settlement will presumably be in the offing after Korea's denuclearization.[307] Russian (and Japanese) officials are deeply concerned about security developments on the peninsula and have made clear their intent to remain engaged with Korean security issues. In addition, Russia's involvement helps mitigate North Korean concerns about becoming overly dependent on China.

In a benign variation of "divide and conquer," American officials should try to deprive their Chinese and Russian counterparts of opportunities to confront the United States jointly. When negotiating divisive issues with these two countries, U.S. representatives should seek the umbrella of an organization in which either China or Russia but not both is a member. For this reason, the NATO-Russian Council or the OSCE provides a better framework than the UNSC for resolving military differences between NATO members and Russia. NATO should consider establishing direct links with China in order to provide enhanced dialogue between the two mutually suspicious but important international actors. Similarly, Russian and Chinese concerns over BMD are best handled bilaterally. In this narrow respect, the exclusion of Russia from the envisaged four-party peace talks regarding the Korean peninsula does have the advantage of discouraging concerted Chinese-Russian action on that issue.

As a general rule, however, Washington should try to include Russia in East Asian institutions and negotiations. Such a policy would recognize that two-thirds of Russia's territory lies in Asia and that many Russians identify their nation as Eurasian. Overtly circumscribing Russia's role in East Asia as a matter of established policy would encourage Moscow to turn toward China. Integrating Russia into East Asia's numerous (though weak) institutions would provide for Russian representation independent of Beijing. On balance, therefore, involving Moscow in any negotiations on a Korean Peace Treaty may well entail advantages that outweigh the associated disadvantages of having to increase the number of negotiating parties, and giving Pyongyang an opportunity to exploit divisions among the other participants.

China's continued exclusion from bilateral Russian-American strategic nuclear arms control negotiations is already impeding U.S.-Russian progress in this area. The Chinese government has traditionally resisted participating in formal nuclear arms control agreements. During the Cold War, Chinese leaders saw superpower nonproliferation initiatives as an attempt to prevent China from developing its own nuclear deterrent. Since then, Beijing has stayed aloof from Russian-American strategic arms talks, arguing that their nuclear arsenals dwarf those of China. Yet the substantial decrease in Russian and U.S. nuclear forces is narrowing this gap. By 2012, Russia and the United States will reduce their strategic nuclear warheads to under 2,000 operational warheads. Depending on the pace of China's future military buildup—which will be determined by many factors beyond the control of Moscow and Washington (e.g., Chinese domestic developments and how the Indian-Pakistani arms race affects Beijing's calculations)—the number of Chinese nuclear warheads could amount to hundreds, putting China on par with Britain and France.

Chinese officials have evinced a growing interest in multinational arms control during the past decade. Although the Chinese remain outside the Russian-American nuclear dialogue, Beijing now supports many international nonproliferation activities. Most recently, China has joined the Global Initiative to Combat Nuclear Terrorism, originally launched by Presidents Bush and Putin on the sidelines of the July 2006 G-8 summit in St. Petersburg. The initiative's prime objective—denying terrorists access to nuclear materials—promotes a goal widely supported by Chinese security experts. Beijing has also undertaken a leading role in cooperating with Russia, the United States, and other countries to secure North Korea's denuclearization. China's expanding arms control horizons suggest an openness to consider novel strategic initiatives.

Involving China and other countries in certain U.S.-Russian arms control processes could facilitate progress between Moscow and Washington in this area and yield ancillary benefits regarding other security issues. For example, if China, India, and Pakistan would subscribe to the Intermediate-Range Nuclear Forces (INF) Treaty, it would reduce the unpredictability of the South Asian arms race, one consequence of which might be to induce Moscow and Washington to hedge substantially against a potential Chinese nuclear buildup. In recent months, Russian officials have been urging joint Russian-U.S. initiatives aimed at transforming bilateral Cold War arms control treaties into multilateral frameworks that could encompass many more countries.[308]

American efforts to dissuade Russia from selling arms to China will have to focus on particularly destabilizing systems. For reasons discussed earlier, the Russians will want to continue to sell weapons to China. A robust U.S. attempt to prevent such arms sales would prove counterproductive. However, cogent strategic analysis demonstrating the need to avoid transferring weapons that could enhance China's ability to project military power far beyond its borders might find a receptive ear in some Russian policymakers who worry about harming Russia's relations with Washington or its Asian allies. In any case, clarifying the quantity and quality of Russian arms sales to China remains exceptionally important, as does securing some type of Western observer presence at future SCO or bilateral military exercises. Chinese and Russian officials need to understand that other countries might respond to the sales and exercises by assuming the worst and increasing their own defense efforts, which in turn could heighten security anxieties in China and perhaps Russia. From such escalatory spirals, dangerous arms races can arise.

Notwithstanding Beijing's past self-exclusion, inviting Chinese representatives to enter into trilateral arms control talks with Russia and the United States might induce their participation, since it would underline China's status as a great power. Important issues warranting trilateral discussions could include reducing strategic nuclear forces, banning ASAT weapons, and especially managing the ballistic missile proliferation that is driving global interest in controversial BMD technologies.

In this regard, U.S. BMD programs should not be permitted even to *appear* to undermine the viability of Russia's or China's nuclear deterrent. That both Russia and China possess secure retaliatory nuclear forces removes a common factor underpinning most military alliances—shared vulnerability. Each state can defend itself, by itself. China's and Russia's assured capacity to launch a retaliatory nuclear strike against the United States or other countries (including each other) allows them—up to a point—to regard U.S. military superiority with a degree of equanimity. No currently envisaged U.S. BMD architecture could negate this capacity, and the quixotic pursuit of one would drive China and Russia closer together.

Although differences persist among governments regarding the nuclear challenge emanating from North Korea and Iran, opportunities exist for greater cooperation even in this divisive area. Recent developments have engendered widespread recognition that the existing nuclear nonproliferation structure requires a major overhaul to deal with the spread of civilian nuclear energy programs and the emergence of transnational proliferation networks operating independently of national governments. In addition, opportunities for national nonproliferation logrolling exist, where Nation A helps mitigate Nation B's proliferation concerns in exchange for Nation B's help in mitigating Nation A's proliferation concerns. Consider the possibilities. Whereas the United States is clearly concerned more than China or Russia about the nuclear aspirations of North Korea and Iran, Russian officials have long worried about Pakistan's role as a proliferator. The Chinese government does not want Japan or Taiwan to develop nuclear weapons, but Chinese security experts have expressed concern that terrorists might acquire a North Korean nuclear explosive device and use it inside China.[309] Most Japanese citizens would still prefer to see a non-nuclear

Japan in a world of few nuclear weapons states rather than a situation in which Japan is one of many nuclear powers. That preference, however, is not immutable.

These cross-cutting concerns mean that opportunities still exist for the world's leading nuclear energy suppliers to cooperate on nonproliferation issues. In particular, there are opportunities to expand American-Chinese-Russian collaboration in the area of developing a more secure global arrangement for supplying nuclear fuel for power generation. At present, Moscow, Washington, and other governments are pursuing parallel but largely independent initiatives to limit the spread of sensitive nuclear technologies, such as uranium enrichment or plutonium reprocessing, by establishing multinational mechanisms that would guarantee uranium fuel supplies to countries that renounce developing their own nuclear fuel manufacturing facilities. A potential avenue for such cooperation would be the U.S.-led Global Nuclear Energy Partnership (GNEP), which seeks to meet growing international demand for civilian nuclear energy while simultaneously promoting the use of more proliferation-resistant reactor technologies.

One complex issue concerns U.S. efforts to promote democracy in Eurasia. On the one hand, Americans' political beliefs and U.S. domestic politics mean that the U.S. Government and American-affiliated nongovernment organizations will ordinarily seek to support Western-style democratic political systems and other civil liberties in Russia, China, and other authoritarian Eurasian countries. On the other hand, aggressive democracy promotion could easily drive the Chinese and Russian political leaders together to defend their regimes. One tactic that might help minimize these invariable tensions is to exploit Russians' general support for democratic political principles and rejection of the "Asian-style" authoritarian political systems. One reason Putin felt obliged to retire from the presidency, rather than join the "president for life club" common in Central Asia, was the widespread Russian belief that he should not rule Russia like an Oriental despot.

When attendees at the February 2008 Munich Security Conference criticized Russia for adopting a Chinese-style one-party political system, First Deputy Prime Minister Sergei Ivanov testily but disingenuously replied that "we don't have a Chinese model. We have a multi-party system."[310] During his speech to the conference, Ivanov stressed that most Russians saw themselves as Europeans, underscoring one advantage the transatlantic community will have over China in competing for Russians' allegiance.[311]

Prudent planning requires preparing for the failure of these shaping policies, especially since their success depends on many factors beyond the immediate control of the U.S. Government. For example, their country's economic and military revival makes Russians more relaxed about China's rising strength in these areas.[312] A return to Brezhnev-era stagnation, or a repeat of the economic and political free fall of the early 1990s, would intensify fears of Russia's becoming a power subordinate to Beijing.

In addition, American policymakers may decide that they must deploy robust BMD systems around parts of Russia's and China's peripheries to deal with threats from Iran and North Korea. Such moves risk inducing Moscow and Beijing to pool their diplomatic and military resources to counter the systems. Any offensive operation against either Tehran or Pyongyang, regardless of its intent, would risk driving China and Russia even more closely together, since such operations would invariably require circumventing the UNSC, where the Chinese and Russian ambassadors could veto any such action. Another wave of color revolutions in Eurasia could also stimulate anti-Western security cooperation between Beijing and Moscow even if Western democracy-promotion efforts contributed little to the upheavals.

The risks of failing to hedge against potential adverse outcomes in relations with China and Russia became evident in 2005. Emboldened by his country's improving ties with Beijing and Moscow, Uzbek leader Islam Karimov abruptly turned against the United States and its allies after they criticized his government for failing to permit an international inquiry into the Andijan crackdown. Western countries then helped persuade Krgyz authorities not compel hundreds of refugees from Andijan to return back to Uzbekistan against their wishes. On July 29, 2005, the Uzbek government instructed U.S. military forces to vacate within 180 days their most important military base in Central Asia, i.e., Karshi-Khanabad (K-2), in southwestern Uzbekistan. One reason for the divided, confused, and largely ineffectual American response to the Andijan massacre was that U.S. officials appear not to have developed contingency plans to cope with such an incident.

Fortunately, many of the best shaping strategies will also position the United States well to respond to adverse developments regarding China and Russia. Sustaining robust forward-based military forces, strengthening security relations with NATO and Japan, and encouraging military transparency and defense spending restraint in China and Russia through arms control will all facilitate an effective U.S. response to any serious deterioration in relations with Beijing and Moscow.

ENDNOTES

1. J. Michael McConnell, "Annual Threat Assessment of the Intelligence Community for the House Permanent Select Committee on Intelligence," February 7, 2008, *www.odni.gov/testimonies/20080207_testimony.pdf.*

2. Peter Spiegel, "Air Force Keeps Eye On Russia, China," *Los Angeles Times,* February 8, 2008.

3. *Ibid.,* as cited.

4. David Lague, "U.S. Military Officials Wary of China's Expanding Fleet of Submarines," *International Herald Tribune,* February 8, 2008.

5. John J. Kruzel, "President Discusses Oppression, Dissent in Run-up to G-8 Summit," American Forces Press Service, *www.defenselink.mil/news/newsarticle.aspx?id=46302.*

6. Dmitri Trenin, *The End of Eurasia: Russia on the Border between Geopolitics and Globalization,* Washington, DC: Carnegie Endowment for International Peace, 2002, p. 221.

7. Cited in Alexander Lukin, *The Bear Watches the Dragon: Russia's Perceptions of China and the Evolution of Russian-Chinese Relations Since the Eighteenth Century,* New York: M. E. Sharpe, 2003, p. 305.

8. Cited in Patrick Moore, "Russia: On the Margins of the Pacific Rim," Radio Free Europe/Radio Liberty, September 11, 2007, *www.rferl.org/feturesarticle/2007/09/6378f428-9a48-43b1-96f8-378267e1b6dc.html .*

9. Cited in Marcel de Haas, "Russia-China Security Cooperation," Power and Interest News Report, November 27, 2006, *www.pinr.com/report.php?ac=view_report&report_id=588&language_id=1.*

10 . State Statistics Committee of Russia, All-Russia Population Census 2002, October 2002.

11. Interfax, "Population of Russian Far East Shrinking by Almost 300 a Day—Envoy," December 20, 2006, *www.interfax.ru/e/B/politics/28.html?id_issue=11650636.*

12. "Heilongjiang," United Nations Economic and Social Commission for Asia and the Pacific (UNESCAP), *http://www.unescap.org/esid/psis/population/database/chinadata/heilongjiang.htm.* See also data for Jilin and Liaoning.

13. Tom Miller, "Reviving Northeast China," September 14, 2005, *www.atimes.com/atimes/China/GI14Ad03.html.*

14. "Survey on Chinese in Russia's Far East," *People's Daily,* January 2, 2004, *english.peopledaily.com.cn/200401/01/eng20040101_131677.shtml.*

15. Vladimir Putin, "Opening Remarks at Security Council Session, December 20, 2006, The Kremlin, Moscow," *www.kremlin.ru/eng/speeches/2006/12/20/1910_type82912type82913_115719.shtml.*

16 . "Survey on Chinese in Russia's Far East."

17 . "Two Chinese Workers Mugged in Russia's Far East," *RIA Novosti,* December 17, 2007.

18. Sergei Blagov, "Russia's Far Eastern Workers Wary of Chinese Migrants," *Eurasia Daily Monitor,* December 18, 2007.

19. Sergei Blagov, "Putin Hopes Hosting APEC Summit Will Spur Development Around Vladivostok," *Eurasia Daily Monitor,* 2007, *www.jamestown.org/publications_details.php?volume_id=420&issue_id=3994&article_id=2371876.*

20. "Fradkov Will Head Commission for Developing Far East," Itar-Tass, February 16, 2007, *www.Itar-Tass.com/eng/level2.html?NewsID=11258149&PageNum=2.*

21. Cited in "Isolation of Russian Far East Threat to National Security-Putin," *RIA Novosti,* December 20, 2006, *en.rian.ru/russia/20061220/57396954.html.*

22. Blagov, "Putin Hopes Hosting APEC Summit Will Spur Development Around Vladivostok."

23. Sergei Blagov, "Russia Weighs Ambitious Plans to Develop Far East," *Eurasia Daily Monitor,* March 5, 2007, *www.jamestown.org/publications_details.php?volume_id=420&issue_id=4024&article_id=2371970.*

24 . "Putin tells Asia: Russia is here to stay," AFP, [n.d.] *afp.google.com/article/ALeqM5ifKblSw23QumSHH6swwafZLLzGOQ.*

25. Blagov, "Russia's Far Eastern Workers Wary of Chinese Migrants."

26 . Vladimir Putin, "Annual Address to the Federal Assembly of the Russian Federation," May 10, 2006, *www.kremlin.ru/eng/speeches/2006/05/10/1823_type70029type82912_105566.shtml.*

27. Zhanna Zayonchkovskaya, "Who Needs Chinese in Russia?" *RIA Novosti,* August 23, 2006, *en.rian.ru/analysis/20060823/53039627.html.*

28. "Russia to Spend $171 mln on Repatriation Program in 2007—Putin," *RIA Novosti,* October 24, 2006, *en.rian.ru/russia/20061024/55088022.html.*

29 . Jean-Christophe Peuch, "Russia's repatriation plan appeals few," Radio Free Europe/Radio Liberty, January 22, 2008, *www.isn.ethz.ch/news/sw/details.cfm?id=18555.*

30. "Russian Quota on Foreign Workers May Result in More Markets Raids," *RIA Novosti,* January 12, 2007, *en.rian.ru/russia/20070112/58967497.html."* The Tajikistan Minister of Labor estimates that up to 800,000 Tajik citizens work in Russia each year, and that at least 80 percent of the Tajik migrants live and work in Russia illegally, "Tajikistan Asks Russia to Set Migrant Worker Quota at 800,000," *RIA Novosti,* January 23, 2007, *en.rian.ru/russia/20070123/59549173.html.*

31. "Russian Quota on Foreign Workers May Result in More Markets Raids."

32 . "No Foreign Traders on Russian Marketplaces from April 1," *RIA Novosti*, April 1, 2007, *en.rian.ru/Russia/20070401/62904938.html.*

33. Henry Meyer, "Russia Set Migrant Quota," Associated Press, *Washington Times,* January 16, 2007.

34. Patrick Moore.

35. Michael Mainville, "Russia Limits Foreign Labor to Fight Illegals," *Washington Times,* January 23, 2007.

36. Putin Urges More Active Measures against Nationalism, Xenophobia," *RIA Novosti,* January 11, 2007, *en.rian.ru/russia/20070111/58897010.html.*

37. "Trade, Economic Cooperation Priorities for Russia, China—Putin," *RIA Novosti,* March 26, 2007, *en.rian.ru/russia/20070326/62647755.html.*

38. The World Bank, Environmental Challenges of Development in the East Asia and Pacific Region, Washington, 2006, p. 2.

39. "A Great Wall of Waste," *The Economist,* August 19, 2004, p. 56.

40. Andreas Lorenz and Wieland Wagner, "China's Poison for the Planet," Spiegel Online, February 1, 2007, *www.spiegel.de/international/spiegel/o,1518,461828-2,00.html;* and Zhong Kaibin, "Crisis Management in China," *China Security,* Winter 2007, pp. 90-109.

41. Jennifer L. Turner, "New Ripples and Responses to China's Water Woes," *China Brief,* Vol. 6, No. 25, December 19, 2006, p. 9.

42. Yu Bin, "China-Russia Relations: Pollution, Politics, and Partnership," *Comparative Connections,* Vol. 7, No. 4, January 2006, pp. 135-136, *www.csis.org/media/csis/pubs/0504q.pdf.*

43. Sergei Blagov, "Russia Concerned by China's Chemical Pollution," *Eurasia Daily Monitor,* Vol. 3, No. 171, September 18, 2006, *www.jamestown.org/edm/article.php?article_id=237145.*

44. *Ibid.*

45. "Joint Statement Between the People's Republic of China and the Russian Federation," April 6, 2007, *www.fmprc.gov.cn/eng/zxxx/t309361.*

46. "China, Russia sign agreement on cross-border water use, protection," *Xinhua,* January 29, 2008, *news.xinhuanet.com/english/2008-01/29/content_7521833.htm.*

47. "Putin proposes 'environmental security system' in Russia," *RIA Novosti,* January 30, 2008.

48. For a summary of the relevant recent polling data, see Dmitry Polikanov, "A Measure of Confidence: What Do Russians Think About China?" October 16, 2006, *www.russiaprofile.org/culture/2006/9/28/4468.wbp;* and Dmitry Shlapentokh, "Unhealthy Competition: Ordinary Russians Fear the Impact of China's Expansion," October 16, 2006, *www.russiaprofile.org/international/2006/10/16/4548.wbp.*

49. See various reports by the EIA available online at *www.eia.doe.gov/.*

50. "Russia's eastern deposits to supply 207 bln cu m of gas by 2030," *RIA Novosti,* December 26, 2007.

51. "Russian gas exports to Asia-Pacific region could top 50 bln cu m," *RIA Novosti,* December 24, 2007.

52. "China and Russia Strengthen Energy Cooperation," China Chemical Reporter, April 6 2007, *www.uofaweb.ualberta.ca/chinainstitute/*; and "China, Russia to Boost Cooperation in Trade, Investment, Energy," Xinhua News Agency, March 27, 2007, *www.uofaweb.ualberta.ca/chinainstitute/.*

53. "Russian PM to Visit China in November—Chinese Ministry," *RIA Novosti,* October 24, 2006, *en.rian.ru/russia/20061024/55092512.html.*

54. "Russia to press ahead with Siberian oil pipe construction," *RIA Novosti,* December 27, 2007.

55. See the map titled, "Power Up Nuclear Reactors in China," based on data provided by the World Nuclear Association, *www.bloomberg.com/apps/data?pid=avimage&iid=iUd8BLclJyvk.*

56. "China to Double Nuclear Power Capacity by 2020," Xinhua, November 16, 2007, *www.chinadaily.com.cn/china/2007-11/16/content_6257821.htm;* and "China to Increase Nuclear Power Capacity," Xinhua, November 3, 2007, *www.chinadaily.com.cn/bizchina/2007-11/03/content_6228767.htm.*

57. Wan Zhihong, "Tianwan to Become Key Power Station," *China Daily,* December 20, 2007, *www.chinadaily.com.cn/bizchina/2007-12/20/content_6334976.htm.*

58. German Gref, "Russian-Chinese Relations: On Right Track," *RIA Novosti,* September 11, 2006, *en.rian.ru/analysis/20060911/53751975.html.*

59. Interfax, cited in Graham Lees, "Hu Returns Home From Russia Empty-Handed on Energy," *World Politics Watch,* March 29, 2007, *www.worldpoliticswatch.com/article.aspx?id=669.*

60. Leon Aron, "After Putin, the Deluge?" *Current History,* Vol. 106, No. 702, October 2007, p. 309.

61. Marshall I. Goldman, "Russia and the West: Mutually Assured Distrust," *Current History,* Vol. 106, No. 702, October 2007, p. 316.

62. Pallavi Aiyar, "More than Neighbours, Less Than Friends?" *The Hindu,* March 26, 2007, *www.uofaweb.ualberta.ca/chinainstitute/.*

63. "Rosneft, Sinopec Discuss Joint Projects," *RIA Novosti,* February 7, 2007, *en.rian.ru/business/20070207/60362154.html.*

64. "China wants Moscow to supply nuclear technology," *Nezavisimaya Gazeta,* December 21, 2007, *en.rian.ru/analysis/20071221/93696018.html.*

65. Cited in "Rosneft Chief Says Oil Supplies to China Can Be Boosted 60 percent," *RIA Novosti*, November 10, 2006, *en.rian.ru/russia/20061110/55513632.html.*

66. Alexandra Gritskova, Konstantin Lantratov, and Gennady Sysoev, "Kitay slozhil rossiyskoe oruzhie" ["China Sets Aside Russian Arms"], *Kommersant*, May 7, 2007.

67. Richard F. Grimmett, Conventional Arms Transfers to Developing Nations,1998-2005, Washington, DC: Congressional Research Service, October 23, 2006, p. 32, *fas.org/sgp/crs/weapons/RL33696.pdf.*

68. For a list of major Russian-Chinese military transactions, see Alyson J. K. Bailes, ed., *SIPRI Yearbook 2006: Armaments, Disarmament, and International Security*, Oxford: Oxford University Press, 2006, pp. 494-495; and Alexandra Gritskova, Konstantin Lantratov, and Gennady Sysoev, "Kak Rossiya vooruzhala Kitay" ["How Russia Has Armed China"] Kommersant, May 7, 2007. Besides the information in the yearbook, the Stockholm International Peace Research Institute maintains a comprehensive record of the Sino-Russian arms trade in its Arms Transfers Database.

69. Grimmett, p. 10.

70. Peter Ford, "Fighter Jet Signals China's Military Advances," *Christian Science Monitor*, January 11, 2007, *www.csmonitor.com/2007/0111/p07s01-woap.htm.*

71. Gritskova, Lantratov, and Sysoev, "Kitay slozhil rossiyskoe oruzhie" ["China Sets Aside Russian Arms"].

72. Marcin Kaczmarski, "Wen Jiabao's Visit To Moscow Fails to Resolve Problems In Russian-Chinese Economic Relations," *CACI Analyst*, November 14, 2007.

73. "Russia-China trade up 44 percent to record $48 bln in 2007," *RIA Novosti*, January 17, 2008, *en.rian.ru/russia/20080117/97148666.html.*

74. Vladimir Ubran, "Posledniy rekord rossiyskogo oruzhiya," Moskovskie Novosti, June 17, 2005. The U.S. Department of Defense also concluded that the Russians might have been exploiting the exercise to show off advanced weapons systems to potential Chinese buyers; see Office of the Secretary of Defense, *Military Power of the People's Republic of China 2006,* Washington, DC: U.S. Department of Defense, 2006, p. 2.

75. Yu Bin.

76. "China Intends to Buy Russia's Su-33," *RIA Novosti,* November 1, 2006, *en.rian.ru/russia/20061101/55289379.html.*

77. Bailes, *SIPRI Yearbook 2006,* p. 454.

78. Cited in "China Intends to Buy Russia's Su-33 Fighters."

79. "Russia Ready to Face Competition on China Arms Market—Official," *RIA Novosti,* November 1, 2006, *en.rian.ru/russia/20061101/55290795.html.*

80. Chzhan Ikhun, "Russko-Kitayskogo torgovlya po oruzhiya razvivaetsya," *Vremya Novostei,* May 27, 2003. For other evidence that Chinese engineers have succeeded in copying Russian military technology for use in China's own defense industry, see Alyson J. K. Bailes, ed., *SIPRI Yearbook 2005: Armaments, Disarmament, and International Security,* Oxford: Oxford University Press, 2005, pp. 423-424.

81. China recently displayed a new supersonic air-launched cruise missile apparently optimized to attack U.S. aircraft carriers. See Joseph E. Lin, "China Unveils New Supersonic Cruise Missile," *China Brief,* Vol. 6, No. 24, December 6, 2006, p. 2.

82. Ivan Safronov, Alexandra Gritskova, and Knstantin Lantratov, "Rossiya Vybiraet mezhdu $1,5 mlrd I $2 mlrd," *Kommersant,* October 30, 2006; and Mure Dickie, Farhan Bokhari, and Arkady Ostrovsky, "China Confident Russia Will Allow Jet Sale," *Financial Times,* November 9, 2006.

83. Leksandra Greitsova and Elena Kiseleva, "Kitayskiye istrebitli doletyat do Pakistana" ["Chinese Fighter Jets to Reach

Pakistan"], *Kommersant*, April 26, 2007, *www.kommersant.ru/doc.aspx?DocsID=762182.*

84. "Co-Production Of Pak-China Thunder Jet JF-17 Begins In Pakistan," *RTI News*, January 22, 2008, *www.freerepublic.com/focus/f-news/1957516/posts.*

85. "Pakistan starts mass production of JF-17 fighters - national TV," *RIA Novosti*, January 22, 2008.

86. Yury E. Fedorov, *"Boffins" and "Buffoons": Different Strains of Thought in Russia's Strategic Thinking*, London: Royal Institute of International Affairs, March 2006, p. 3, *www.cfr.org/content/publications/attachments/BP0306russia.pdf.*

87. Dmitri Trenin, "Russia's Threat Perception and Strategic Posture," in *Russian Security Strategy under Putin: U.S. and Russian Perspectives*, Carlisle, PA: Strategic Studies Institute, U.S. Army War College, November 2007, p. 47.

88. For a detailed list of China's major military exchanges with Russia in 2005, see *China's National Defense in 2006*, Beijing, China: Information Office of the State Council, December 29, 2006, Appendix II, *www.fas.org/nuke/guide/china/doctrine/wp2006.html.*

89. For additional information on the exercise, see Office of the Secretary of Defense, *Military Power of the People's Republic of China 2006*, Washington, DC: U.S. Department of Defense, 2006, p. 2; Mikhail Lukin, "Peace Mission 2005: A 1970s Template for Sino-Russian 'Peacekeeping'," *Moscow Defense Brief*, No. 2, 2005, pp. 15-18; and "Russia-China Security Cooperation," *PINR News Report*, November 27, 2006, *www.pinr.com/report.php?ac=view_report&report_id=588&language_id=1.*

90. "President Hu Jintao Holds Talks with His Russian Counterpart Putin," Ministry of Foreign Affairs of the People's Republic of China, March 27, 2007, *www.fmprc.gov.cn/eng/zxxx/t306902.htm.*

91. "Joint Statement Between the People's Republic of China and the Russian Federation," April 6, 2007, *www.fmprc.gov.cn/eng/zxxx/t309361.*

92. *Ibid.*

93. See, for example, their "Joint Declaration on International Order in the Twenty-First Century" that Presidents Putin and Jintao signed on July 1, 2005, and the 5th anniversary summit declaration of the Shanghai Cooperation Organization that they and the other SCO leaders signed the following July.

94. Christopher Marsh and Nikolas K. Gvosdev, "China's Yugoslav Nightmare," *The National Interest*, Summer 2006.

95. Citations in Colum Lynch, "Russia, China Veto Resolution on Burma," *Washington Post,* January 13, 2007.

96. "Politika SShA provotsiruet novuyu gonku vooruzheniy, schitayut v Minoborony" ["The Ministry of Defense Believes that U.S. Policies Are Provoking a New Arms Race"], January 20, 2007, *www.rian.ru/world/foreign_russia/20070120/59422900.htm.*

97. Saurabh Das, "Putin Slams U.S. Space Weapons," Associated Press, *Moscow Times,* January 26, 2007.

98. Associated Press, "Russia, China take Joint Stance Against US," Turkish Daily News, February 14, 2007, *www.turkishdailynews.com.tr/article.php?enewsid=66176.*

99. Igor Gaidar, "Yadernyy balans: opasnye igri," Vedomosti, March 30, 2006. The controversial article asserting that the U.S. strategic buildup was in the process of negating Russia's and China's nuclear deterrents was that of Keir A. Lieber and Daryl G. Press, "The Rise of U.S. Nuclear Primacy," *Foreign Affairs*, March/April 2006.

100. Gaidar.

101. Yurii Baluyevskiy, "Pro Soedinnyx shtatov: shot dal'she?: Komu I zachem nuzhen protivoraketnyy zontik," *Voenno-Promishlenniy Kur'er*, July 26, 2006.

102. Vladimir Putin, "Speech and the Following Discussion at the Munich Conference on Security Policy," February 10,

2007, *www.kremlin.ru/eng/speeches/2007/02/10/0138_type82912type82914type82917type84779_118135.shtml.*

103. Cited in "Russian Expert Opposes U.S. Missile System," United Press International, January 31, 2007, *www.upi.com/NewsTrack/Top_News/2007/01/31/russian_expert_opposes_us_missile_system/;* see also Nikolai Khorunzhy, "Who Can Europe-Based Missiles Threaten?" October 17, 2006, *en.rian.ru/analysis/20061017/54890694.html.*

104. Andrei Kislyakov, *RIA Novosti,* "Missile Defense and Its Consequences," February 15, 2007, *en.rian.ru/analysis/20070215/60788503.html.* Lavrov's comments are in *RIA Novosti,* "German FM Calls for Civilized Dialogue on U.S. Missile Shield," February 22, 2007, *en.rian.ru/world/20070222/61126427.html.*

105. See, for example, "Russia's FM Urges U.S. to Hold Broader Consultations on Missile Defense in Europe," March 21, 2007, AP, *www.kyivpost.com/bn/26314/.*

106. See, for example, Valdimir Simonov, "U.S.-Russia: Consultations or Simple Notification?" *RIA Novosti,* March 19, 2007, en.rian.ru/analysis/20070319/62218403.html; and Viktor Litovkin, "US BMD Case Cuts No Ice," *RIA Novosti,* April 10, 2007.

107. Cited in Martin Sieff, "Russia claims BMD-proof missile," United Press International, May 30, 2007, *www.upi.com/Security_Terrorism/Analysis/2007/05/30/bmd_watch_russia_claims_bmdproof_missile/6487/.*

108. See, for example, "Russia Will Be Able to Hit NMD Elements, if They Are Deployed in Europe—Official," February 19, 2007, Interfax, *www.interfax.ru/e/B/0/28.html?id_issue=11681055;* "Russian Bombers Could Suppress U.S. Missile Shield—General," *RIA Novosti,* March 5, 2007, *en.rian.ru/world/20070305/61569829.html;* and "Russia Could Respond to U.S. Radar in Caucasus—Air Force Chief," *RIA Novosti,* March 2, 2007, *en.rian.ru/russia/20070302/61470806.html.*

109. Richard Weitz, *Russian-American Security Cooperation after St. Petersburg: Challenges and Opportunities*, Carlisle, PA: Strategic Studies Institute, U.S. Army War College, 2007.

110. Joseph E. Lin and Christopher Griffin, "Cold War Redux: China Responds to the Russo-American BMD Dispute," *China Brief*, July 11, 2007, *www.jamestown.org/china_brief/article.php?articleid=2373540.*

111. "Foreign Ministry Spokesperson Liu Jianchao's Remarks on Russia's Suspension of its Participation in the CFE Treaty," *capetown.chineseconsulate.org/eng/fyrth/t342466.htm.*

112. Lin and Griffin.

113. Chinese Ministry of Foreign Affairs, "Foreign Ministry Spokesperson Liu Jianchao's Remarks on Russia's Suspension of its Participation in the CFE Treaty," *http://www.fmprc.gov.cn/ce/cgmb/eng/fyrth/t342466.htm.*

114. William Choong, "Moscow Queries Aussie Role in US Missile Defence," *The Straits Times*, September 26, 2007.

115. "Russia Says Iran Poses No Threat," *RIA Novosti*, August 16, 2007, *en.rian.ru/russia/20070816/71949222.html.*

116. "China to Join Hands with Russia in Mars Mission," November 8, 2008, *chinadigitaltimes.net/2008/02/beijing-and-moscow-to-propose-joint-space-treaty.*

117. The document is available at *www.ostp.gov/html/US percent20National percent20Space percent20Policy.pdf.*

118. Chinese concerns are surveyed in Jing-Dong Yuan, "China Eyes U.S. Space Policy," *WMD Insights*, March 2006, *www.wmdinsights.org/I3/EA1_China_Eyes_US.htm.*

119. Stephanie Nebehay, "China, Russia to Offer Treaty to Ban Arms in Space," January 25, 2008, *www.reuters.com/article/worldNews/idUSL2578979020080125?feedType=RSS&feedName=worldNews.*

120. Associated Press, "Russia Warns U.S. about Weapons in Space," *USA Today*, June 2, 2005.

121. Vladimir Popovkin, "Russia's Space Defenses Stage a Revival," October 4, 2006, *en.rian.ru/analysis/20061004/54509604.html.*

122. Associated Press, "Russian Official Sharply Criticizes Assertive New U.S. Space Policy," *International Herald Tribune,* November 29, 2006.

123. "Russia, China challenge US with proposal to ban space weapons at disarmament conference," Associated Press, February 12, 2008, *www.iht.com/articles/ap/2008/02/12/news/Disarmament-Space-Weapons.php.*

124. Cited in Associated Press, "Russia-China Space Pact Won't Include Key Technology," December 26, 2006, *www.cnn.com/2006/TECH/space/12/26/russia.china.space.ap/index.html.*

125. Alexander Khramchikhin, "Privet iz Kitaya" ["Greetings from China"], Izvestia, February 12, 2007.

126. "FSB Accuses Scientist of Leaking Missile Secrets to China-1," *RIA Novosti,* May 24, 2007, *en.rian.ru/russia/20070524/66057837.html;* and "Russia Says Suspect Sold China Rocket Technology," Reuters, May 24, 2007, *www.defensenews.com/story.php?F=2783624&C=asiapac.*

127. Theresa Hitchens, U.S.-Sino Relations in Space: From 'War of Words' to Cold War in Space?" *China Security,* Winter 2007, pp. 18-19.

128. Bill Gertz, "U.S. Halts China Space Ventures," *Washington Times,* February 2, 2007.

129. "Russia Speaks for Broader Space Cooperation with U.S.-Lavrov," *RIA Novosti,* February 3, 2007, *en.rian.ru/world/20070203/60160879.html.*

130. Dina R. Spechler and Martin C. Spechler, "Trade, Energy, and Security in the Central Asian Arena," in Ashley J. Tellis and Michael Wills, eds., *Strategic Asia 2006-07: Trade, Interdependence, and Security,* Seattle, WA: 2006, p. 225.

131. Erica Marat, "Russia Decreases Immigration Quota Threefold in 2008," *CACI Analyst,* January 9, 2008, *www.cacianalyst.org/?q=node/4771.*

132. Nicholas Schmidle, "In Central Asia, New Players, Same Game," *Washington Post,* January 29, 2006.

133 "Die meisten Staatschefs sprachen russisch," [Most Chiefs of State Speak Russian], Frankfurter Allgemeine Zeitung, April 30, 2001, cited in F. Stephen Larrabee and Ian O. Lesser, *Turkish Foreign Policy in an Age of Uncertainty,* Santa Monica, CA: RAND, 2003, p. 102.

134. Richard Weitz, "Central Asia: Looking At Language Politics," *Eurasia Insight,* January 28, 2008, *www.eurasianet.org/departments/insight/articles/eav012808a.shtml.*

135. Andrew McGregor, "Chinese Counter-Terrorist Strike in Xinjiang," *CACI Analyst,* March 7, 2007.

136. Igor Rotar, "The Growing Problem of Uighur Separatism," China Brief, April 15, 2004. For a detailed analysis of the Uighur issue, see Matthew Forney, "One Nation-Divided," *Time International,* March 25, 2002, pp. 38-41; Graham E. Fuller and S. Frederick Starr, *The Xinjiang Problem,* Washington, DC: Central Asia-Caucasus Institute, Paul H. Nitze School of Advanced International Studies, 2004; and "Under the Thumb: China's Far West," *The Economist,* U.S. edition, December 3, 2005, pp. 52-55. The rise and decline of the anti-Beijing insurgency in Xinjiang is discussed in Chien-Peng Chung, "The Defense of Xinjiang," *Harvard International Review,* Vol. 25, No. 2, Summer 2003, pp. 58-62.

137. "Chinese Parliament Okays Anti-Terrorism Pact with Neighbours," *The Press Trust of India,* October 28, 2004. For a review of how Kazakhstan has tried to meet Beijing's concerns regarding Xingjian, and Taiwan, see Marat Yermukanov, "Chinese

Conundrum of Kazakhstan's Multi-Vector Policy," *Central Asia-Caucasus Analyst,* July 13, 2005, www.cacianalyst.org/view_article.php?articleid=3463.

138. Kathleen Moore, "Central Asia: China's Mounting Influence, Part 4—Facing Militant Threats," November 18, 2004, *www.rferl.org/featuresarticle/2004/11/d541f15b-c660-4310-8afd-33c787f5ecae.html.*

139. Chietigj Bajpaee, "China's Quest for Energy Security," *ISN Security Watch,* February 25, 2005, *www.isn.ethz.ch/news/sw/details.cfm?ID=10840.*

140. Roger N. McDermott, "Kazakhstan's Emerging Security Ties with China," *CACI Analyst,* September 5, 2007.

141. "China ascendant in new 'Great Game' over Central Asian riches," Associated Press, December 14, 2007, *www.iht.com/articles/ap/2007/12/14/asia/AS-FEA-GEN-Kazakhstan-Chinas-Great-"Game.php.*

142. "Back to the Great Game," *Indian Express*, June 4, 2006.

143. Isabel Gorst, "Kazakhstan and China Sign Pipelines Deal," *Financial Times,* August 20, 2007, *www.ft.com/cms/s/0/a0a8f722-4e7f-11dc-85e7-0000779fd2ac.html.*

144. Farkhad Sharip, "China Secures New Access to Kazakh Oil," *Eurasia Daily Monitor,* circa December 20, 2006.

145. United Press International, "Sinopec to Invest $106M in Uzbek Oil," July 20, 2005, *www.washingtontimes.com/upi/20050720-035907-2529r.htm.*

146. "Shanghai Cooperation Organization Summit Opens," June 15, 2006, *www.rferl.org/featuresarticle/2006/06/6BAB21AD-B9D7-4FD0-94EC-3DD956F85C7C.html.*

147. Erkin Ahmadov, "Sino-Uzbek Relations and The Energy Politics Of Central Asia," *CACI Analyst,* November 14, 2007.

148. John C. K. Daly, "Beijing Raises Stakes in Turkmen Gas Game," *Eurasia Daily Monitor,* November 1, 2007.

149. Daniel Kimmage, "2005 in Review: The Geopolitical Game in Central Asia," *RFE/RL Central Asia Report,* Vol. 5, No. 49, December 30, 2005, *www.rferl.org/featuresarticle/2005/12/509208c8-5d99-481b-8a52-e121e4bd664d.html.*

150. Russell Ong, "China's Security Interests in Central Asia," *Central Asian Survey,* December 2005, Vol. 24, No. 4, December 2005, p. 432.

151. "China plans rail link to Central Asia for oil," January 1, 2008, *business.uzreport.com/mir.cgi?lan=e&id=42174.*

152. Zhao Huaheng, "China, Russia, and the United States: Prospects for Cooperation in Central Asia," *CEF Quarterly: The Journal of the China-Eurasia Forum,* February 2005, p. 24, *www.silkroadstudies.org/new/docs/CEF/CEF_Quarterly_Winter_2005.doc.pdf.*

153. Niklas Swanstrom, "China and Central Asia: A New Great Game or Traditional Vassal Relations?" *Journal of Contemporary China,* Vol. 14, No. 15, November 2005, pp. 579-580.

154. Su Qiang, "SCO nations pledge closer partnership," *China Daily,* August 17, 2007, *www.chinadaily.com.cn/china/2007-08/17/content_6030530.htm.*

155. "China ascendant in new 'Great Game' over Central Asian Riches."

156. Stephen Blank, "China's Recent Energy Gains In Central Asia: What Do They Portend," *CACI Analyst,* October 31, 2007.

157. "New railways to link China's Xinjiang with central Asia," Xinhua, January 27, 2008, *news.xinhuanet.com/english/2008-01/27/content_7501969.htm.*

158. "Fear of the Dragon," *The Economist,* November 11, 2004, *www.economist.com/PrinterFriendly.cfm?story_id=3376598.*

159. For an assessment of the factors driving the Russian decision not to resist the deployment of substantial U.S. military forces in Central Asia immediately after the 9/11 attacks, see George Friedman, *America's Secret War: Inside the Hidden Worldwide Struggle between America and its Enemies,* New York: Doubleday, 2004, pp. 141-149; and Andrew S. Weiss, "Russia: The Accidental Alliance," in Daniel Benjamin, ed., *America and the World in the Age of Terror: A New Landscape in International Relations,* Washington, DC: Center for Strategic and International Studies, 2005, pp. 125-150.

160. For expressions of growing dissatisfaction with the U.S. military presence among senior Russian officials even before the color revolutions, see Roy Allison, "Strategic Reassertion in Russia's Central Asia Policy," *International Affairs,* London, Vol. 80, No. 2, 2004, pp. 278-280, 292-293.

161. "Russian Foreign Ministry Against Enforcement of Democracy," *Vedomosti,* August 17, 2005, reprinted *www.russiaprofile.org.*

162. Agence France Presse, "Putin Takes Swipe at US Policy in Central Asia," June 15, 2006, *archive.turkishpress.com/news.asp?id=128802.*

163. Cited in Dilip Hiro, "Shanghai Surprise," June 16, 2006, *commentisfree.guardian.co.uk/dilip_hiro/2006/06/shanghai_surprise.html.*

164. Jason Kelly, "Anti-Terrorism with Chinese Characteristics: Peace Mission 2007 in Context," *China Brief, www.jamestown.org/china_brief/article.php?articleid=2373758.*

165. "Russia Faces Major Security Challenge in the East, Official Says," *RIA Novosti,* June 6, 2006, *en.rian.ru/russia/20060606/49101912.html.*

166. China's military modernization program along its western border is discussed in Stephen Blank, "The Central Asian Dimension of Chinese Military Strategy," *China Brief,* Vol. 4, No. 10, May 13, 2004, *www.jamestown.org/publications_details.php?volume_id=395&issue_id=2952&article_id=23670;* and Martin

Andrew, "Guarding the West: China's New Mechanized Infantry Division," *China Brief, www.jamestown.org/china_brief/article.php?articleid=2373403.*

167. Cited in "Beijing Mulls Central Asian Military Deployment," *China Reform Monitor,* June 20, 2005. Chinese reaction to the "Tulip Revolution" is evaluated in Zamir Chargynov, "Revolution, Repression, and Re-election in 2005: China's Response to Political Developments in Central Asia," *Chian and Eurasia Forum Quarterly,* Vol. 4, No. 1, February 2006, pp. 31-32.

168. For more on the Russian reaction, see Dmitri Trenin, "Russia and the Shanghai Cooperation Organization: A Difficult Match," *CEF Quarterly: The Journal of the China-Eurasia Forum,* July 2005, p. 26, *www.silkroadstudies.org/new/docs/CEF/CEF_Quarterly_July_2005.pdf.*

169. ITAR-TASS, "Kyrgyzstan Won't Have Chinese Military Base on it Territory," July 29, 2005. Evidence of possible Chinese interest in establishing such bases, and Russia's presumed opposition to such a development, are discussed in Stephen Blank, "China Joins the Great Central Asian Base Race," *Eurasia Insight,* November 16, 2005, *www.eurasianet.org/departments/insight/articles/eav111605.shtml.*

170. Igor Tomberg, "Energy Outcome of SCO Meeting in Dushanbe," September 20, 2006, *en.rian.ru/analysis/20060920/54104304.html.*

171. Nicklas Norling and Niklas Swanström, "Sino-Russian Relations in Central Asia and the SCO," *CACI Analyst,* October 3, 2007.

172. Pan Guang, "China and Central Asia: Charting a New Course for Regional Cooperation," *China Brief, www.jamestown.org/china_brief/article.php?articleid=2373267.*

173. For descriptions of these exercises, see Roger N. McDermott and William D. O'Malley, "Countering Terrorism in Central Asia," *Jane's Intelligence Review,* Vol. 15, No. 10, October 2003, pp. 16-19; Robert Sae-Liu, "China Looks Outward with its

Exercise Programme," *Jane's Defence Weekly*, September 24, 2003; and Jing-dong Yuan, "Anti-Terror Exercises Only a First Step," *Moscow Times*, August 14, 2003.

174. Cited in Michael Mainville, "Central Asian Bloc Considering Iran for Membership," *Washington Times*, June 5, 2006.

175. "SCO Member-States Hold Anti-terrorism Exercises in Uzbekistan," UzReport.com in English, March 10, 2006, *jahon.mfa.uz/modules.php?op=modload&name=News&file=article&sid=2202&mode=thread&order=0&thold=0&POSTNUKESID=1a2788d7b8af4f13ae1ee52d22602e6c*.

176. Xinua, "Declaration on 5th Anniversary of SCO," June 15, 2006, *news.xinhuanet.com/english/2006-06/15/content_4703117.htm*.

177. SCO Secretariat, "Declaration of Heads of Member States of Shanghai Cooperation Organisation," July 5, 2005, *www.sectsco.org/news_detail.asp?id=500&LanguageID=2*.

178. Cited in Ann Scott Tyson, "Russia and China Bullying Central Asia, U.S. Says," *Washington Post*, July 15, 2005.

179. Alexander Gabuyev and Bek Orozoliyev, "Киргизия разворачивает американские самолет" ["Kyrgyzstan Turns Back American Aircraft"], *Kommersant*, May 25, 2007, *www.kommersant.ru/doc.html?docId=768505*.

180. Erica Marat, "As SCO Summit Approaches, Kyrgyz Government Caught Between Russia, U.S.," E*urasia Daily Monitor*, June 14, 2007, *www.jamestown.org/edm/article.php?article_id=2372230*.

181. "U.S. Military Presence in Central Asia Complicated by Regional Rivalry," *International Herald Tribune*, June 1, 2007, *www.iht.com/articles/ap/2007/06/01/asia/AS-GEN-Kyrgyzstan-US-Base.php*.

182. Erica Marat, "U.S. Urges Kyrgyzstan to Continue Bilateral Cooperation against Terrorism," *Central Asia-Caucasus Analyst*, June 13, 2007, p. 18.

183. Bruce Pannier, "Kyrgyzstan: U.S. Defense Secretary Seeking Support for Air Base," June 5, 2007, *www.rferl.org/featuresarticle/2007/06/bf660efd-739d-418e-98eb-662a6d1dc642.html.*

184. Stephen Blank, "New Turns in Chinese Policy towards Central Asia," *Central Asia-Caucasus Analyst,* June 15, 2005, *www.cacianalyst.org/view_article.php?articleid=3371;* and Daniel Kimmage, "Central Asia: SCO—Shoring Up the Post-Soviet Status Quo," July 8, 2005, *www.rferl.org/featuresarticle/2005/07/9a8d1c5f-b72b-4a40-aedc-08ed11aaa34f.html.*

185. For an example of their contrasting assessments of SCO members' elections, see Daniel Kimmage, "Analysis: Kyrgyz, Tajik Elections Present Familiar Issues, New Context," March 2, 2005, at *www.rferl.org/featuresarticle/2005/3/0CC368CF-94C7-48A9-A904-006F8864A975.html.*

186. Jason Kelly, "Anti-Terrorism with Chinese Characteristics: Peace Mission 2007 in Context," *China Brief, www.jamestown.org/china_brief/article.php?articleid=2373758.*

187. Tim Johnson, "Russia, China, and allies play war game," *Seattle Times,* August 11, 2007, *seattletimes.nwsource.com/html/nationworld/2003831600_asia11.html.*

188. Alim Seytoff, "SCO exercise aimed at suppressing Uighurs," *www.atimes.com/atimes/China/IH16Ad06.html.*

189 "Russia, China Presence on CentAsia Energy Market-View," *ITAR-TASS,* August 22, 2007, *www.Itar-Tass.com/eng/level2.html?NewsID=11807153&PageNum=0.*

190. Dmitry Kosyrev, "Rush Demand for Shanghai Cooperation Organization," *RIA Novosti,* August 17, 2007, *en.rian.ru/analysis/20070817/72171635.html.*

191. "Azerbaijan Interested in Ties with SCO—Official," August 25, 2007, *www.interfax.ru/e/B/politics/28.html?id_issue=11844997.*

192. "Nepal: Looking For Observer Status In Shanghai Organization," *www.telegraphnepal.com/news_det.php?news_id=1813.*

193. Cited in Rowan Callick, "Iran Welcome in China's New Sphere," *The Australian,* June 13, 2006.

194. "No Basis for SCO Enlargement Yet Developed," June 6, 2006, *www.interfax.com/3/163064/news.aspx.*

195. Anna Smolchenko and Nabi Abdullaev, "SCO Seeks Deeper Energy Ties," *Moscow Times,* August 16, 2007, p. 5, *www.themoscowtimes.com/stories/2007/08/16/041.html.*

196. "Moratorium on Admission to Shanghai Six to Hold-FM Lavrov," *RIA Novosti,* August 16, 2007, *en.rian.ru/world/20070816/71927153.html.*

197. David L. Stern, "Iran Leader Denounces U.S. Missile Shield Plan," August 16, 2007, *www.iht.com/articles/2007/08/16/news/summit.php.*

198. Cited in Kosyrev.

199. Warren Hoge, "China and Russia Stall Sanctions on North Korea," *New York Times,* October 13, 2006. The resolution also authorized the establishment of a committee to monitor the implementation of the sanction. See "UN Security Council Resolution 1718 on North Korea," October 14, 2006, *www.state.gov/p/eap/rls/ot/76180.htm.*

200. Bonnie Glaser, "U.S.-China Relations: Dialogue Boosts Ties, Even Without Results," *Comparative Connections,* March 2007, Vol. 8, No. 4, p. 36, *www.csis.org/media/csis/pubs/0604qus_china.pdf.*

201. "Russian Diplomat Says Nuclear-Armed North Korea is a Threat to Russia," *International Herald Tribune,* January 31, 2007, *www.iht.com/bin/print.php?id=4416788.*

202. Cited in Scarlett Lim, "Russian Amb. Ivashentsov Stresses Russia Will Assist Inter-Korean Business Ties," *Seoul Times,* February 5, 2007, *theseoultimes.com/ST/?url=/ST/community/foreign_missions/foreign_missions.html.*

203. "Six Nations to Wrap Up N. Korea Nuclear Talks," *RIA Novosti,* February 13, 2007, *en.rian.ru/world/20070213/60629950.html.*

204. Assessments of China's policies toward North Korea include You Ji, "Understanding China's North Korea Policy," *China Brief,* Vol. 4, No. 5, March 3, 2004, pp. 1-3; David Shambaugh, "China and the Korean Peninsula: Playing for the Long Term," *The Washington Quarterly,* Vol. 26, No. 2, Spring 2003, pp. 43-56; and "Intelligence Brief: China's Policy toward North Korea Remains Unchanged," *Power and Interest News Report,* March 12, 2007, www.pinr.com/report.php?ac=view_report&report_id=568&language_id=1. For information on Russia's policies, see Alexander Vorontsov, "Current Russia-North Korea Relations: Challenges and Achievements," CNAPS Working Paper Series, February 2007, *www.brook.edu/fp/cnaps/papers/vorontsov2007.htm.*

205. "North Korea gives G8 nations new ammunition against U.S. missile defense system," CNN, August 22, 2000. transcripts.cnn.com/TRANSCRIPTS/0007/22/smn.02.html.

206. According to press reports, the Russian government agreed to back a UNSC resolution denouncing the DPRK's nuclear test in return for U.S. acceptance of a Security Council resolution criticizing the Georgian government for pursuing policies Moscow opposed. See Column Lynch, "U.N. Near Agreement on N. Korea Sanctions," *Washington Post,* October 13, 2006.

207. "Russia-N Korea Trade Down to USD 209 mln in 2006-Official," March 5, 2007, *www.Itar-Tass.com/eng/level2.html?NewsID=11308395&PageNum=0.*

208. "Russia-N. Korea Trade Turnover Down 13 percent in 2006," *RIA Novosti,* March 5, 2007, *en.rian.ru/world/20070305/61595495.html.* An official in the Russian Ministry of Finance said that "Russia has proposed different debt settlement options to North Korea, including debt for investment, debt for property. But North Korea claims it has legislative restrictions against implementing Russian proposals," cited in *RIA Novosti,* "Russia Hope for Quick Settlement to N. Korea's Debt-FM Lavrov," March 6, 2007, *en.rian/Russia/20070306/61633963.html.* For a history of the Russian-DPRK

debt issue, see Sergei Blagov, "Russia Mulls North Korean Debt Write-Off," *Eurasia Daily Monitor*, January 22, 2007.

209. Ivan Safronov et al., "Russia to Write Off 80 Percent of North Korean Debt-Newspaper," January 5, 2007, *www.mosnews.com/news/2007/01/05/koreadebt.shtml*.

210. James Clay Moltz, paper presented at the 13th annual International Security Conference of Sandia National Laboratories, "International Security Challenges and Strategies in the New Era," April 23-25, 2003, Albuquerque, New Mexico, *cns.miis.edu/research/korea/ruspol.htm*.

211. Sergei Blagov, "Moscow Eyes Coordination with China over North Korean Test," *Eurasia Daily Monitor*, October 16, 2006, *www.jamestown.org/edm/article.php?article_id=2371543*.

212. Vladimir Putin described the problems in the Russian Far East in a recent public speech. See "Opening Remarks at Security Council Session, December 20, 2006, The Kremlin, Moscow," *www.kremlin.ru/eng/speeches/2006/12/20/1910_type82912type82913_115719.shtml*. Russian Foreign Minister Sergey Lavrov said that successful Six-Party talks would, by removing an impediment to East Asian peace and prosperity, help advance "the development of Russia's Far East and Siberia regions." See "South Koreign Foreign Minister Visits Moscow for N. Korean Talks," *Pravda*, March 6, 2007, *english.pravda.ru/news/world/06-03-2007/88036-south-korea-0*.

213. Like their Chinese counterparts, Russian policymakers oppose two other possible models—employing considerable economic sanctions and other nonmilitary pressure, as with Libya, or armed intervention to seize WMD sites, as in Iraq; Yong-Chool Ha and Beom-Shik Shin, Russian Nonproliferation Policy and the Korean Peninsula, Carlisle Barracks, PA: Strategic Studies Institute, U.S. Army War College, December 2006, pp. 5-8.

214. "Putin Optimistic on North Korea," October 27, 2006, *St. Petersburg Times*, *www.sptimes.ru/index.php?action_id=2&story_id=19283*. Putin used the "corner" argument in answering a question posed during his appearance at the February 2007 Munich Conference on Security Policy. See "Speech and the Following Discussion at the Munich Conference on Security Policy."

215. Anne Wu, "What China Whispers in North Korea's Ear," *The Washington Quarterly,* Vol. 28, No. 2, Spring 2005, pp. 35-48.

216. Edward Cody, "Tentative Nuclear Deal Struck with North Korea," *Washington Post,* February 13, 2007. The text of the agreement is reprinted on the website of *The Korea Times, times.hankooki.com/lpage/nation/200702/kt2007021320383011990.htm.*

217. Steven R. Weisman and Donald Greenless, "U.S. Discusses Releasing North Korean Funds," *New York Times,* March 1, 2007.

218. For a range of estimates, see Tim Johnson, "Nuclear Accord Far From Foolproof, Experts Fear," *Miami Herald,* February 18, 2007.

219. For divergent assessments of the February 2007 accord, see Helene Cooper and Jim Yardley, "Pact with North Korea Draws Fire From a Wide Range of Critics in U.S.," *New York Times,* February 13, 2007; Glenn Kessler, "Conservatives Assail North Korea Accord," *Washington Post,* February 15, 2007; Bruce Klingner, "North Korea Nuclear Weapons Agreement Falls Short," Heritage Foundation WebMemo #1358, February 13, 2007, www.heritage.org/Research/AsiaandthePacific/wm1358.cfm; George Perkovich, "Imperfect Progress," *Wall Street Journal,* February 14, 2007; and "Dealing with North Korea: Trust me?" *The Economist,* February 15, 2007, *www.economist.com/opinion/displaystory.cfm?story_id=8702881.*

220. Cited in David E. Sanger, "Outside Pressures Snapped Korean Deadlock," *New York Times,* February 14, 2007. Former Bush administration officials have claimed that its strategy had always been to approach the North Korean nuclear issue as an opportunity to promote wider regional cooperation and resolve problems persisting since the Korean War. See, for example, Robert B. Zoellick, "Long Division," *Wall Street Journal,* February 26, 2007; and Philip Zelikow, "The Plan That Moved Pyongyang," *Washington Post,* February 20, 2007.

221. Esther Pan, "South Korea's Ties with China, Japan, and the U.S.: Defining a New Role in a Dangerous Neighborhood," Council on Foreign Relations, February 8, 2006, *www.cfr.org/publication/9808/#5.*

222. "North Korea Will Move Towards Reform Despite Nukes, Says Roh," February 27, 2007, *www.channelnewsasia.com/stories/afp_asiapacific/view/260869/1/.html.*

223. Blagov, "Russia Mulls North Korean Debt Write-Off."

224. Analysts forecast that the percentage of Russian oil flowing to Asia will increase from 3 percent today to at least 30 percent by 2020. See, for example, Peter Rutland, "Russia's Economic Role in Asia: Toward Deeper Integration," in Tellis and Wills, eds., *Trade, Interdependence, and Security,* p. 182. See also the statements of Putin and other Russian government officials in "Russia to Drastically Raise Oil Exports to Asia-Pacific—President," *RIA Novosti,* September 17, 2006, *en.rian.ru/russia/20060917/53969376.html.*

225. "China Surpasses U.S. to Become Japan's Largest Trading Partner," *Asahi Shimbun,* April 26, 2007, *www.asahi.com/english/Herald-asahi/TKY200704260104.html.*

226. Wendell Minnick, "Military Hot Line Will Link China and Japan," *Defense News,* April 19, 2007, *defensenews.com/story.php?F=2697141&C=asiapac.*

227. For a summary of the dispute, see Kent E. Calder, "China and Japan's Simmering Rivalry," *Foreign Affairs,* Vol. 85, No. 2, March/April 2006, pp. 130-131; and Anthony Faiola, "Japan-China Oil Dispute Escalates," *Washington Post,* October 22, 2005.

228. Japan Asks China to Halt Gas Output in Disputed Field," *Bloomberg.com,* February 1, 2007, *www.bloomberg.com/apps/news?pid=newsarchive&sid=ajwyqMzkXUU0.*

229. An extensive description of China's growing military capabilities appears in the annual U.S. Department of Defense reports to Congress on Chinese military power. See, for example, *Annual Report to Congress: Military Power of the People's Republic of China 2006,* Washington, DC: Office of the Secretary of Defense, 2006, *www.defenselink.mil/pubs/pdfs/Chinapercent20Reportpercent202006.pdf.* See also Michael Armacost, "The Mismatch between Northeast Asian Change and American Distractions," *NBR Analysis,* Vol. 18,

No. 1, January 2007, p. 8, *www.nbr.org/publications/analysis/pdf/vol18no1.pdf.*

230. Japan Defense Agency, "Summary / Tentative Translation," *Defense of Japan 2005,* Tokyo, 2005, p. 13, *www.mod.go.jp/e/index_.htm.*

231. The CIA estimates that China's military expenditures in 2005 amounted to $81.4 billion; see U.S. Central Intelligence Agency, *World Factbook,* Washington, DC: 2006. Some observers place China's aggregate defense spending as high as $450 billion. see Ed Feulner, "A New Arms Race America Must Win," *Chicago Sun-Times,* April 18, 2007. Forecasts of future Chinese military spending are offered in Keith Crane et al., *Modernizing China's Military: Opportunities and Constraints,* Santa Monica, CA: RAND, 2005. The methodological difficulties in analyzing China's defense spending are assessed in Richard A. Bitzinger, "Just the Facts, Ma'am: The Challenge of Analysing and Assessing Chinese Military Expenditures," *China Quarterly,* No. 173, March 2003, pp. 164-175.

232. China's National Defense in 2006. See also Willy Lam, "China Outlines Ambitious Objectives in Its Defense White Paper," *China Brief,* Vol. 7, No. 1, January 10, 2007, pp. 2-3.

233. Jim Yardley and David Lague, "Beijing Accelerates its Military Spending," *New York Times,* March 5, 2007.

234. For a comprehensive assessment of China's military buildup, see David Shambaugh, "China's Military Modernization: Making Steady and Surprising Progress," in *Strategic Asia 2005-06: Military Modernization in an Era of Uncertainty,* Seattle, WA: National Bureau of Asian Research, 2005, pp. 67-103.

235. Divergent evaluations of Taiwan's ability to deter or defeat a PLA military attack appear in Michael A. Glosny, "Strangulation from the Sea? A PRC Submarine Blockade of Taiwan," *International Security,* Vol. 28, No. 4, Spring 2004, pp. 125-160; Michael O'Hanlon, "Why China Cannot Conquer Taiwan," *International Security,* Vol. 25, No. 2, Fall 2000, pp. 51-86; and David Shambaugh, "A Matter of Time: Taiwan's Eroding Military Advantage," *Washington Quarterly,* Vol. 23, No. 2, Spring 2000, pp. 119-133.

236. Mariko Sanchanta and Mure Dickie, "Japan Pushes for Naval Visits to Bolster China Ties," *Financial Times,* January 23, 2007.

237. Ministry of Foreign Affairs of Japan, "Japan-China Joint Press Statement, Provisional Translation," April 11, 2007, *www.mofa.go.jp/region/asia-paci/china/pv0704/joint.html.*

238. Richard Weitz, "A Military Hot Line Would Mean Little," *International Herald Tribune,* April 8, 2007.

239. John H. Miller, "Russia-Japan Relations: Prisoners of History?" October 2004, p. 2, Asia-Pacific Center for Security Studies, *www.apcss.org/PublicationsSAS/AsiaBilateralRelations/Japan-Russia RelationsMiller.pdf.*

240. These are summarized in Andrei Ivanov, "Yaponiya podelila kurily nadvoe" ["Japan Divides Kurils in Half"], *Kommersant,* October 24, 2007, *www.kommersant.ru/doc.aspx?DocsID=818129.*

241. Glenn E. Curtis, ed., *Russia: A Country Study,* Washington, DC: U.S. Library of Congress, 1996, *countrystudies.us/russia/85.htm.*

242. James Brooke, "Japan and Russia, With an Eye on China, Bury the Sword," *New York Times,* February 13, 2005, *www.yale.edu/japanus/Articles/NYTimes2.13.05.htm.*

243. "Japan seeks return of fishermen," August 18, 2006, *news.bbc.co.uk/2/hi/asia-pacific/5262566.stm.*

244. "Russian Bomber Violated Airspace, Japan Says," *International Herald Tribune,* February 9, 2008, *www.iht.com/articles/ap/2008/02/09/asia/AS-GEN-Japan-Russia-Intrusion.php.*

245. "Russia denies Japan's spying allegations," *RIA Novosti,* January 16, 2008.

246. "Tokyo activists stage anti-Russian protests amid spy scandal," *RIA Novosti,* January 17, 2008.

247. Prime Minister of Japan and His Cabinet, Japan-Russia Summit Meeting, November 21, 2005, *www.kantei.go.jp/foreign/koizumiphoto/2005/11/21nichiro_e.html.*

248. Huang Jilian, "Taiwanese Studies in Russia," *Russian Studies,* No. 3, 1995, *jds.cass.cn/Article/20060516154913.asp.*

249. "Pay Attention to Russian and Taiwan," *Xinhua,* July 5, 2007, *www.1911.cn/Article/ShowArticle.asp?ArticleID=9669.*

250. Huang Jilian.

251. Czeslaw Tubilewicz, "The Little Dragon and the Bear: Russian-Taiwanese Relations in the Post-Cold War Period," *Russian Review,* Vol. 61, No. 2, April 2002.

252. "Russia for one China, against Taiwan's independence-ministry," *RIA Novosti,* July 23, 2007; and "Russia opposed to "UN membership under the name Taiwan," *Xinhua,* July 24, 2007, *news.xinhuanet.com/english/2007-07/24/content_6420065.htm.*

253. "India's Nuclear Tests Show Fear of China," *Wall Street Journal,* May 15, 1998, p. 13.

254. Jing-Dong Yuan and Arjun Dutta, "China-India Defense Memorandum of Understanding Well Received," *WMD Insights,* No. 7, July/August 2006, *www.wmdinsights.com/I7/I7_SA2_ChinaIndiaDefense.htm.*

255. Jehangir S. Pocha, "In China, Nuclear Pact Creates Concern," *Boston Globe,* March 3, 2006.

256. Martin Sieff, "Defense Focus: India buys T-90s-Part 3," January 17, 2008, *www.upi.com/International_Security/Industry/Analysis/2008/01/17/defense_focus_india_buys_t-90s_–_part_3/6092*

257. "Indian PM's Visit," China Daily, January 14, 2008, *www.chinadaily.com.cn/opinion/2008-01/14/content_6391191.htm.*

258. "A Shared Vision for the 21st Century," *china-japan21.org/eng/zxxx/t399545.htm.*

259. Harsh V. Pant, "India's Interests at Stake in Relationship with China," *www.pinr.com.*

260. Strobe Talbot, E*ngaging India: Diplomacy, Democracy, and the Bomb,* Washington, DC: Brookings Institution, 2004.

261. For more on this strategy, see Christopher J. Pehrson, *String of Pearls: Meeting the Challenge of China's Rising Power Across the Asian Littoral,* Carlisle Barracks, PA: Strategic Studies Institute, U.S. Army War College, July 2006.

262. Chietigj Bajpaee, "India, China Locked in Energy Game," *Asia Times,* May 17, 2005, *www.atimes.com/atimes/Asian_Economy/GC17Dk01.html.*

263. Evan S. Medeiros, "Strategic Hedging and the Future of Asia-Pacific Stability," *The Washington Quarterly,* Vol. 29, No. 1, Winter 2005-06, p. 156.

264. Abbas Milani, "Russia and Iran: An Anti-Western Alliance," *Current History,* Vol. 106, No. 702, October 2007, p. 332.

265. Sanam Vakil, "Iran: Balancing East against West," *The Washington Quarterly,* Vol. 29, No. 4, 2006, pp. 51-65.

266. Robert O. Freeman, "Russian-Iranian Relations in the 1990s," *Middle East Review of International Affairs,* Vol. 4, No. 2, June 2000, p. 68.

267. Edmund Herzig, "Iran and Central Asia," in Roy Allison and Lena Jonson, eds., *Central Asian Security: The New International Context,* Washington, DC: Brookings, 2001, pp. 174-178.

268. "Putin: Gazprom Ready to Join Iran-Pakistan-India Pipeline Project," June 17, 2006, *www.turkishdailynews.com.tr/article.php?enewsid=46456.*

269. Cited in Rowan Callick, "Shanghai Group's Power Play," *The Australian,* June 16, 2006.

270. "Regional Security Summit Vows to Ensure Stability in Asia," *RIA Novosti,* August 16, 2007, *en.rian.ru/world/20070816/71908472.html.*

271. Gentry, J. Brandon, "The Dragon and the Magi: Burgeoning Sino-Iranian Relations in the 21st Century," *The China and Eurasia Forum Quarterly,* Vol. 3, No. 3, November 2005, pp. 114-115.

272. Neil King, Jr., "China-Iran Trade Surge Vexes U.S.," *Wall Street Journal,* July 27, 2007.

273. China-Iranian ties as they relate to Central Asia are discussed in Frederick Stakelback, "The Growing Tehran-Beijing Axis," *National Interest,* January 4, 2005, *www.inthenational interest.com/Articles/Januarypercent202005/January2005stakelbeck.html.*

274. "Putin, Hu Talk Iran, North Korea, SCO, Space Security in Moscow," *RIA Novosti,* March 26, 2007.

275. "Russia Says Iran Poses No Threat."

276. George Jahn, "Officials: Russia Ups Pressure on Iran," *The Guardian,* August 7, 2007, *www.guardian.co.uk/worldlatest/story/0,6833348,00.html.*

277. "Guarded views on Putin Proposal for Azerbaijan Missile Shield," *Tehran Times,* June 11, 2007, *http://www.tehrantimes.com/Index_view.asp?code=143326.*

278. Permanent Mission of the Russian Federation to the United Nations Office and other International Organizations in Geneva, "Excerpts from Transcript of the Direct Line of the President of the Russian Federation Vladimir Putin with the President of Russia Live Television and Radio Broadcast," October 24, 2007, *www.geneva.mid.ru/speeches/53.html.*

279. "Vladimir Putin's First Visit to Iran," *RIA Novosti,* October 15, 2007, *www.cdi.org/russia/johnson/2007-215-25.cfm.*

280. A few years ago, estimates of Caspian oil were substantially higher. See R. Craig Nation, "U.S. Interests in the New Eurasia,"

in *Russian Security Strategy under Vladimir Putin: U.S. and Russian Perspectives,* Carlisle Barracks, PA: Strategic Studies Institute, U.S. Army War College, November 2007, pp. 9-10.

281. Neil King, Jr., "China-Iran Trade Surge Vexes U.S.," *Wall Street Journal,* July 27, 2007.

282. "Russia, China, France Blast Opening of Iraq War," PBS Online NewsHour, March 20, 2003, *www.pbs.org/newshour/updates/worldreaction_3-20.html.*

283. "Russian Minister of Foreign Affairs Sergey Lavrov, Interview with the Syrian Arab News Agency," March 1, 2007. *www.un.int/russia/new/MainRoot/docs/off_news/020307/newen1.htm.*

284. Yufeng Mao, "Beijing's Two-Pronged Iraq Policy," *China Brief,* May 24, 2005, *www.jamestown.org/publications_details.php?volume_id=408&issue_id=3344&article_id=2369791.*

285. Yufeng Mao, "Beijing's Two-Pronged Iraq Policy," *China Brief,* May 24, 2005, *www.jamestown.org/publications_details.php?volume_id=408&issue_id=3344&article_id=2369791.*

286. Judy Aita, "U.N. Security Council Backs Multinational Force in Iraq," USINFO, July 14, 2007, *usinfo.state.gov/xarchives/display.html?p=washfile-english&y=2007&m=June&x=20070614124810atiayduj0.9642603.*

287. "Foreign Ministry Spokesman Qin Gang's Regular Press Conference," December 7, 2006, *www.fmcoprc.gov.mo/eng/gsxwfb/lxjzzfh/t282948.htm.*

288. Edith M. Lederer, "Security Council Expands Iraq Role," Associated Press, August 10, 2007, *www.time.com/time/world/article/0,8599,1651889,00.html.*

289. "A Quintet, Anyone?" *The Economist,* January 11, 2007, *www.economist.com/world/asia/displaystory.cfm?story_id=8521894.*

290. Bill Gertz, "China Arms Both Sides," *Washington Times,* July 27, 2007.

291. Demetri Sevastopulous, "US concerns over China weapons in Iraq," *Financial Times*, July 6, 2007, *www.ft.com/cms/s/82ce0740-2c03-11dc-b498-000b5df10621,dwp_uuid=17aab8bc-6e47-11da-9544-0000779e2340.html.*

292. "China takes aim at US over claims Chinese missiles are in Iraq," Agence-France Presse, July 26, 2007, *www.iraqupdates.com/p_articles.php/article/19950.*

293. "China agrees to cancel Iraqi debt," *Xinhua*, June 21, 2007, *www.chinadaily.com.cn/china/2007-06/21/content_899679.htm.*

294. "Moscow Backs Lukoil Iraq Project," *Financial Times*, April 25, 2007, *www.iraqdirectory.com/DisplayNews.aspx?id=3672.*

295. *Ibid.*

296. Steve Negus, "Iraq To Consider Reviving Saddam-Era Oil Deal," *Financial Times*, February 12, 2008, *www.ft.com/cms/s/0/b0452282-d980-11dc-bd4d-0000779fd2ac.html?nclick_check=1.*

297. M. K. Bhadrakumar, "China Plays its Own Energy Game," *Asia Times Online*, December 19, 2006, *www.atimes.com/atimes/China/HL19Ad06.html.*

298. "Russian Diplomats 'To Be Killed'," BBC, June 21, 2006, *news.bbc.co.uk/2/hi/middle_east/5102532.stm.*

299. "Russia Says Its Embassy in Iraq Raked With Gunfire," Reuters, January 11, 2007, *www.alertnet.org/thenews/newsdesk/L11626791.htm.*

300. Mark N. Katz, "Policy Watch: Russia's Middle East Strategy," *World Peace Herald*, June 11, 2007, *wpherald.com/articles/5126/2/Policy-Watch-Russias-Middle-East-strategy/Chechen-worries.html.*

301. Aita.

302. Russian Minister of Foreign Affairs Sergey Lavrov, Interview with the Syrian Arab News Agency, March 1, 2007, *www.un.int/russia/new/MainRoot/docs/off_news/020307/newen1.htm.*

303. Mark N. Katz, "Policy Watch: Russia's Middle East Strategy," *World Peace Herald,* June 11, 2007, *wpherald.com/articles/5126/2/Policy-Watch-Russias-Middle-East-strategy/Chechen-worries.html.*

304. Michael J. Green, "America's Quiet Victories in Asia," *Washington Post,* February 13, 2007; and Sheng Lijun, "Beijing's Soft Power in Southeast Asia," *International Herald Tribune,* January 17, 2007.

305. At various points, prominent Germans, Japanese, Taiwanese, and commentators in other U.S. allied countries have given serious thought to acquiring nuclear weapons as a hedge against security abandonment by the United States. See, for example, Campbell et al., *Nuclear Tipping Point,* Washington, DC: Brookings, 2004.

306. See, for example, Sergei Lavrov, "One Cold War Was Enough," *Washington Post,* February 25, 2007; or President Bush's statement cited in "Bush Seeks Cooperation with Russia Despite Putin's Harsh Remarks," February 15, 2007, *english.pravda.ru/world/americas/15-02-2007/87423-Bush_cooperation_Russia-0.*

307. U.S. Department of State, "Interview with KBS TV: Christopher R. Hill, Assistant Secretary for East Asian and Pacific Affairs," Seoul, Korea, February 5, 2007, *www.state.gov/p/eap/rls/rm/2007/80131.htm.*

308. Cited in "Ivanov says Russia and U.S. Must Take Lead on New Arms Regime," Reuters, February 10, 2008, *uk.reuters.com/article/worldNews/idUKL1030195520080210?feedType=RSS&feedName=worldNews.*

309. Eric A. McVadon, "Beijing's Frustrations on the Korean Peninsula," *China Brief,* Vol. 7, No. 4, February 21, 2007, p. 9.

310. Mark John, "West need not fear resurgent Russia: Ivanov," Reuters, February 10, 2008, *uk.reuters.com/article/worldNews/idUKL1030398720080210?feedType=RSS&feedName=worldNews.*

311. Sergey B. Ivanov, "Where is Russia heading? New Vision of Pan-European Security," February 10, 2008, *www.securityconference.de/konferenzen/rede.php?menu_2008=&menu_konferenzen=&sprache=en&id=217&.*

312. Christopher Marsh, "Russia Plays the China Card," *The National Interest,* November-December 2007.

ABOUT THE AUTHOR

RICHARD WEITZ is a Senior Fellow and Director of Program Management at the Hudson Institute. His current areas of research include defense reform; counterterrorism; nonproliferation; homeland security; and U.S. policies towards Europe, Asia, and the former Soviet Union. Dr. Weitz currently serves as head of the Case Studies Working Group of the Project on National Security Reform. He previously worked for the Department of Defense and other public policy research institutes. Dr. Weitz is the author of *The Reserve Policies of Nations: A Comparative Analysis* (Strategic Studies Institute, U.S. Army War College, 2007), and *Revitalising US–Russian Security Cooperation: Practical Measures* (Routledge, 2005), and has coedited *Mismanaging Mayhem: How Washington Responds to Crisis* (Praeger Security International, 2008). His commentaries have appeared in the *International Herald Tribune, Washington Times,* and other publications. Dr. Weitz holds degrees from Harvard, Oxford, and the London School of Economics.